How to Plan and Plant
Your Own Property

How to
PLAN AND PLANT

Planting Plans by the author

**Photographs by Molly Adams
except as noted**

YOUR OWN PROPERTY

by Alice Recknagel Ireys,
Landscape Architect

William Morrow & Company, Inc.
New York, 1975

Printed in the United States of America.

1   2   3   4   5   79   78   77   76   75

Library of Congress Catalog Card Number 67-19689

ISBN 0-688-06831-6 (pbk.)

To the loving memory of my husband
and for my children—
Catherine, Anne, and Henry

Acknowledgments

I wish to express my appreciation to all who have helped to make this book possible.

To clients and friends whose places are illustrated; nurserymen and contractors for their concern and interest.

To my good friend, Clara Coffey, who has given me continued encouragement and help.

To my secretary, Ann Morrison, who has patiently typed many pages of the manuscript.

To Howard Abel, who has redrawn my plans for this publication.

To the photographers, particularly Molly Adams and Louis Buhle, for their help in capturing with cameras the design features essential for illustration.

Insofar as possible the botanical names used throughout this book follow *Hortus Second* compiled by L. H. Bailey and Ethel Zoe Bailey (Macmillan, New York, 1946).

Contents

Part I

Fundamentals

What are the best shade trees? How can we plant for privacy so near the street? What hedges don't need clipping? Are there evergreens that stay small? What plants are right for a house in the woods? Will anything grow beside a windswept seashore cottage?

Owners of old and new properties repeatedly ask these and many other questions. Sometimes the answers are simple; usually they are complex for there is much more to this than stopping by a roadside stand in spring and picking up a few plants that appeal to you. What is involved is planting design—the selection of proper plants for various parts of your property and grouping them into pleasing compositions. The shape and character of each plant in relation to its neighbors, its color and texture, its function in the overall plan—these are important factors in the development of a good general design. Also to be considered are the climatic and soil conditions of your site so that what you plant will thrive.

In much the same way that an artist works on canvas to produce a painting, you work to create a three-dimensional design that will please you when you look out a window or walk around your property. Of course, landscape design differs from painting in that its purpose is to produce a living functional picture as well as a beautiful one. The picture that you create will change from season to season and from year to year for plants rarely remain exactly the same.

To create an attractive enduring picture, you need to understand the fundamentals of designing a property and how to use plants to get the effect you want. It is necessary to apply basic principles of scale, proportion, unity, balance, and rhythm to your whole scheme and then to select material that will carry out and strengthen your design. You will need to employ imagination as well as knowledge; when a plan is well visualized, the result is exciting and rewarding.

Characteristics of plants

Scale of a plant concerns its use in relation to its surroundings. For example, trees may be selected to frame a house, give shade to a terrace, or hide an objectionable view. The elm, a large-scale tree, looks well for a Georgian house, and healthy elms are becoming possible again. The flowering dogwood at the corner is in good scale. An alternate planting might be a red maple, *Acer rubrum,* for the elm, and a showy crabapple, *Malus floribunda,* for the dogwood.

The form of a plant should be recognized before it can be used to best advantage. Has it the domelike shape of beech or horsechestnut? The pyramid of fir, hemlock, or holly? The weeping aspect of most willows? Try to train your eye to recognize the different forms of plants.

Texture depends on size of leaves, the way they are attached to stems, and the surface quality of foliage as a whole—whether rough or smooth, dull or shiny, thick or thin. Foliage texture serves to create mood and gives a sense of movement and light to a landscape. For example, the oak suggests strength with its heavy textured bark and leaves, while the honey locust offers grace and lightness.

Color of foliage is affected by its texture, and this is important in planning a composition. Trees with many leaves close together appear to be one color; those with open foliage have shadows and appear to be of two or more colors. Consider the autumn tints of deciduous trees as well as the winter effect of evergreens, particularly the range of greens in hollies and junipers.

Color of flowers in trees and shrubs is another consideration. Since flowers are seasonal as well as showy, think about color harmonies. You might combine flame, bronze, orange, and buff azaleas in a striking composition but you would then avoid introducing pinks and magentas.

Design elements

Proportion is the pleasing relationship of one part of a composition to another—and to the whole. As you arrange your groups on paper, consider each plant—its size at maturity, its relation to the overall design. Two mistakes can be seen everywhere—the crowded shrub border—overgrown and no longer in proportion to a property—and the small house buried in arborvitae. You will discover that most plants grow faster and require wider spacing than you realize at the start.

Unity in a composition is achieved with plants of related form, color, and texture. Don't plan a garden or a boundary with such a hodge-podge that the eye is impelled to move restlessly from one plant to another.

Balance, symmetrical or asymmetrical, is necessary for a sense of stability. Trees and shrubs evenly arranged around a central feature, as a grass panel or pool, will be in symmetric balance. A front door that is not centered needs asymmetric treatment, as a shadbush on one side with three low-growing yews on the other.

Rhythm in design is gained by repeating the same plant or group of plants, and rhythm gives a sense of movement. In a small garden, you might repeat the star magnolia at regular intervals, and there will be a sense of progression. Or you might select plants that have the same qualities—as the different hollies—and then repeat them in rhythmical groupings with other plants. Avoid using a great variety of plants.

The climax of your design will be something that demands attention, a focal point, requiring plants of special interest. Here, unusual and often expensive specimens count the most.

Guides to planning

Study the fascinating subject of landscape design; and work out a general design for your property that takes into account the needs and interests of your family.

Look at plants until you know what characteristics each can contribute to your plan.

Try to analyze the good garden designs you see, and discover what makes them attractive. No two places are ever exactly alike and you can learn a great deal—and with pleasure—through observation and analysis.

The elm—a large-scale tree like the red and sugar maples, the pin oaks and honey-locusts—is well suited to this large Georgian house. BUHLE PHOTO

2.
How to Make a Planting Plan

From your deed survey, you can obtain a plot plan showing the dimensions of your property. With this as guide, transfer dimensions and house location to graph or cross-section paper marked off in little squares. Let each square represent a foot; 1 inch to 10 feet is a workable scale. First mark the North Point. Then on the house outline, indicate doors and windows; on the open spaces, existing trees, walls, fences, septic tanks, oil pipes, and any other elements that may affect your design as views you wish to enjoy or objects you want to conceal.

Existing trees may be shown by a dot; try to locate them exactly by measuring on the ground the distance from two corners of the house to the center of each tree. Using the two measurements, with a compass swing an arc on your plan; this will indicate the position of any tree.

If there is considerable change of grade, you may need a topographical survey that will show differences in levels, rock outcrop, and other physical features. Knowing what exists on your property is essential.

Next make a list of what you and your family want. Probably you cannot include everything but you can determine priorities. Then work out a landscape plan that includes what you have and what you want. You may need professional help with this. A trained mind and a trained eye can give you considerable assistance through the initial phases of designing and can also save you time and costly mistakes. A plan made by a landscape architect can be your guide for years to come. With this plan—and some knowledge of plants—you can go a long way on your own in developing an attractive landscape design. If you cannot afford a plan, even one consultation on the ground will help you analyze your problems and get you started in the right direction.

Once you have a general design, you can study it as a whole with planting in mind. Decide where you want to emphasize a vista or screen an objectionable view, and where shade is needed. This first step is a study of composition rather than of detail and may be worked out roughly on tracing paper. Perhaps you will make several sketches before you get one that appeals to you.

As you work over your plan, try to think in three dimensions. Consider plants—their lines, light, scale, color, and texture—not as single specimens but in relation to the whole. Remember they will not look the same in every season. In winter you will have one picture with evergreens dominant, in spring shrubs will be in bloom, in autumn leaves will be a blaze of color. Mark on your plan the types of plants, as tall deciduous trees or low evergreens, that will fill the desired function, be in scale, and also adapted to prevailing conditions of soil and light.

Plan of a small plot showing existing material.

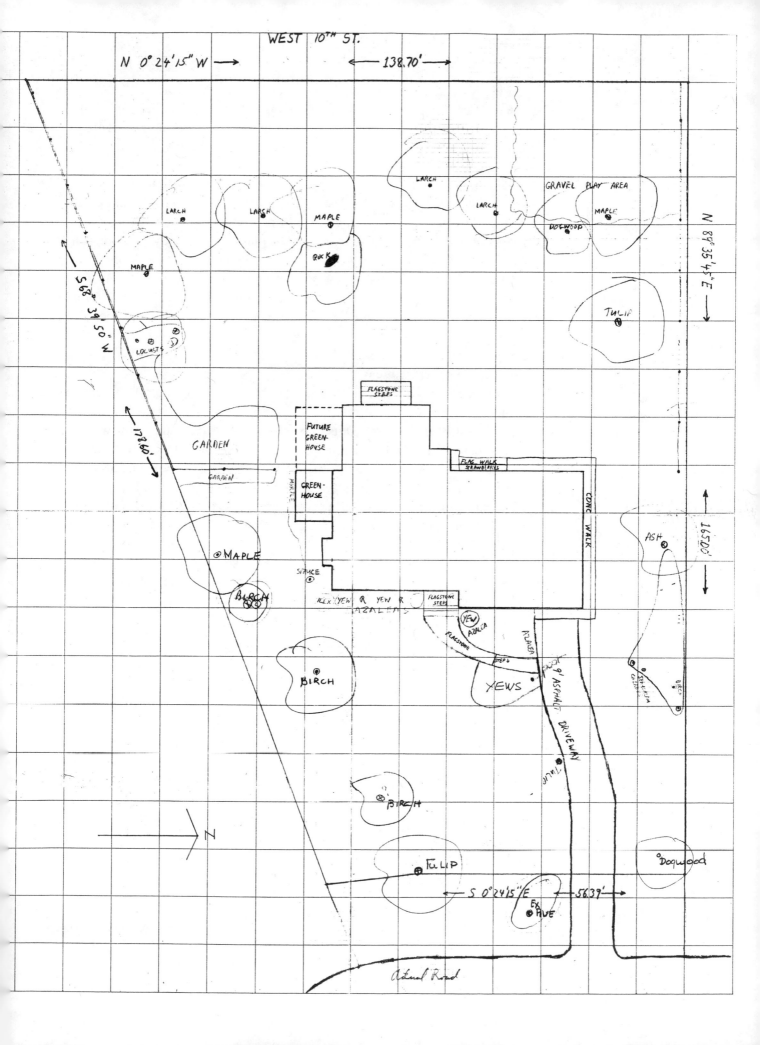

Finally, you come to plant compositions and garden details. Remember you are creating pictures not developing a botanical collection. I had a friend who bought one each of every plant listed in the catalogue of Wayside Gardens; she had a fascinating collection but hardly the makings of a garden.

And now about your budget. Can you afford immediate effects or will you have to wait, perhaps five years, for your plants to complete your design? If you are just starting out and plan to live in your house for some years, you can begin with very small plants and enjoy watching them develop. Too often people want an "instant" effect and this results in overcrowding. In a few years, unless some plants are removed, the whole effect is ruined. Proper spacing is important at the start. Plants need room to grow; try to find out the spread of each at maturity and be guided accordingly.

The three important areas

Approach area. Here plants should be interesting in all seasons. For winter you can have evergreens, for spring and summer a few flowering trees, in fall their colorful fruits. Try to select with restraint; you want your home to have a dignified setting. What this will include depends upon the architecture, as well as your taste and desires. Some houses have a long driveway with a formal courtyard that needs large-scale planting; others adjacent to the street, may have room for just a few plants in front. Modern houses sometimes have an overhang so wide that plants cannot live underneath.

In each case it is important to relate house and grounds; the house should appear to belong to its site. Perhaps flowering trees at the corners will bring the two together. Perhaps a great expanse of bare wall can be minimized with vines or espaliers.

Outdoor living areas. Most of your property will be for this purpose with terraces, lawn areas, gardens, play spaces, and maybe a pool. The right plants will enhance each situation while contributing to the attractiveness of the whole. You may select shrubs for a flowering boundary, tall evergreens for backgrounds, or a specimen shade tree. Trees are of first concern because most of them grow slowly. Next comes the planting around terrace and nearby areas. A well-graded lawn, adequate for your property, but not overwhelming in upkeep, will give dignity to your outdoor living areas.

Selecting proper plants for each section, knowing the forms, foliage, and flowers, as well as ultimate heights, takes time. All this is part of making a planting plan.

Plan indicating layout and spacing.

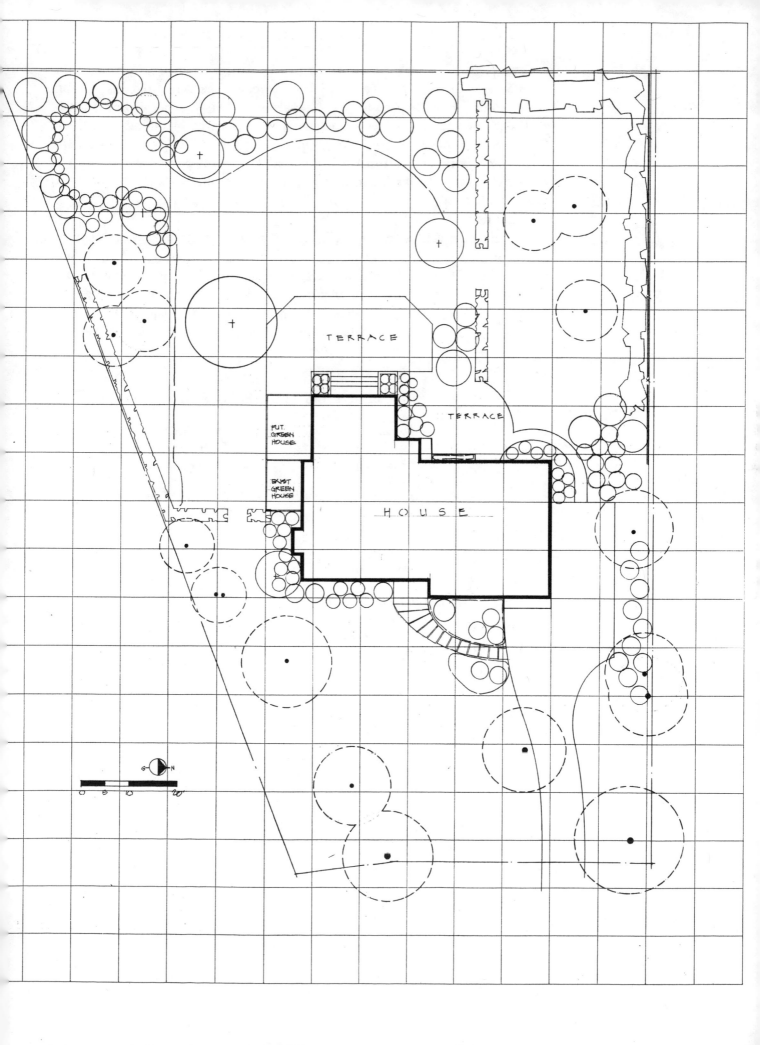

TERRACE

TERRACE

FUT.
GREEN
HOUSE

EXIST
GREEN
HOUSE

H O U S E

S N

0 5 10 20'

Service area. This may include a vegetable garden, orchards, flowers for cutting, or just space for a compost pile. It can be concealed by a fence, hedge, or shrubs. I like to include here two early blooming plants, the winter honeysuckle, *Lonicera fragrantissima,* and the pussywillow, *Salix discolor.* Form and texture are not perfect in these two but they are colorful in February and March and nice to cut then for early bouquets.

Plant lists

With plan completed, to facilitate ordering, itemize the plants you want under these headings: Quantity, Botanical Name, (Common Name), Size, Remarks. On your list group trees, then shrubs, vines, groundcovers, and lastly, the herbaceous material which includes flowers. You can then send this list to nurseries for estimates, or use the catalogue of a nearby nursery to estimate for yourself. Add charges for delivery and planting; these may

PLANT LIST FOR ESTIMATE

Trees

2	*Cornus florida*	8–9' matched specimens
1	*Kousa chinensis*	7–8' multiple-stemmed
1	*Gleditsia triacanthos*	2–2½" cal. branched high
1	*Ilex opaca*	5–6'
1	*Malus floribunda Arnoldiana*	6–7' branched low
8	*Tsuga canadensis*	4–5' not trimmed

Shrubs

20	*Azalea* 'Gumpo'	1–1½'
	'Rose Greeley'	1½–2'
5	*mollis*	2–3' selected colors
3	*Ilex Aquifolium Aquiperni*	2–3'
6	*crenata*	2–3'
9	*convexa*	1½–2'
30	*glabra*	1½–2'
20	*Kalmia latifolia*	2–3'
6	*Pieris japonica*	2–3'
1	*Pyracantha coccinea Lalandii*	pot 6"
10	*Rhododendron* 'Boule de Neige'	1½–2'
4	*maximum*	2–3'
30	*Taxus media Hatfieldii*	2–3'
5	*baccata repandens*	1½–2' spread
18	*Vaccinium corymbosum*	2–3'
3	*Viburnum prunifolium*	3–4'

Ground cover

150	*Pachysandra terminalis*	3" pot
150	*Vinca minor*	3" pot

Finished planting plan that can be carried out over several years.

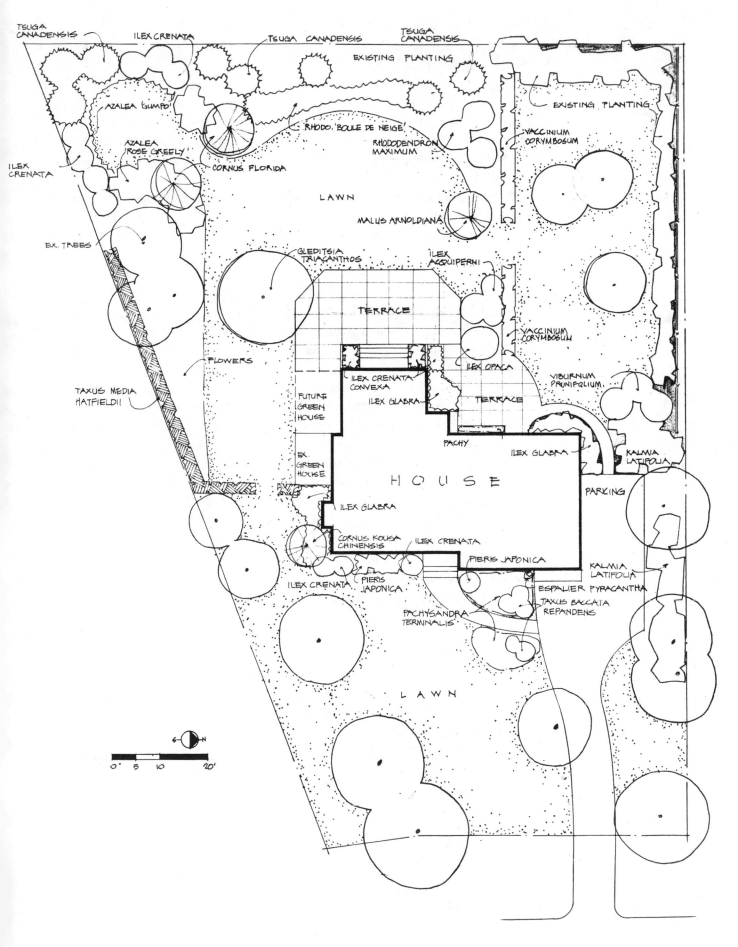

run as high as fifty percent of the plant costs. At the end of this chapter is the kind of list I send out.

From your plan, marked out in feet, you can determine the number of plants you need. Familiarize yourself with botanical names and order by these. Common names mean different plants to different people. If you ask for a syringa, you may get a lilac, a mock-organge, or a spirea, but if you specify *Syringa vulgaris,* you will get just one thing, the common purple lilac.

Order trees by caliper—the diameter of the trunk 1 foot above the ground —other material by height or spread. Under remarks indicate whether you want a tree, high-branched, double-trunked, or perhaps a pair of matched specimens.

As a follow-up to an accepted estimate, visit your nursery and mark the plants you want. Your nurseryman can be helpful in selecting good material and he can introduce you to unfamiliar plants or new cultivars. Over the years I have gained a great deal of knowledge from the nurserymen who grow their own plants. These dedicated plantsmen are interested in giving the public well-grown and suitable trees and shrubs. If you want unusual material, make your wishes known to your local nurseryman. He will try to grow or find what you want and in turn you will help to create a demand for the out-of-the-ordinary plants that make gardens more interesting.

Selecting plants is difficult for most people. In winter it is a temptation to order too many evergreens; you forget that in spring you will want flowering trees and shrubs, in fall some interesting berries. Then there are the plant catalogues to cope with. Everything sounds so enticing; it is a temptation to overorder but resist the urge and follow your plan exactly. If you are interested in collecting plants, give over space to a little nursery of your own where you can line-out small specimens that you want to evaluate before giving them a permanent place.

Four guides

Study the layout of your property as a whole. Select plants that have a function and that also fit into the design.

Study the need for evergreens, deciduous masses of varying heights and spreads, the screening of unsightly views.

Observe the climate and soil of your property. Be aware of shade, sun, and drainage conditions for all these affect your selection.

Consider the cost of first planting and of future maintenance. If you are holding to a budget, the detailed plan will permit you to work in stages. Then the completed design will be pleasing and unified.

Your house needs a pleasant, welcoming entrance whether it is at the end of a long curving driveway or just a short distance from the street. A proper place to park and an easy way to the front door are essential. For the friendly approach you want a path that is direct, obvious, well-paved, wide enough for two people to walk comfortably side-by-side, and attractively planted. Select plants that require no unsightly winter protection, that will look well throughout the year.

In planting the approach, consider the architecture of your home, the natural surroundings, and the kind of material that will give artistic effect and also grow well in your locality. Need for privacy may require a hedge along the street or an enclosed front garden. Much of this is a matter of personal preference, of designing your place to suit you.

Styles in architecture

If you are dealing with a house of definite style, your problem is comparatively easy. Much has been written about appropriate plantings for colonial, Spanish, or other specific types. But your house may be of no particular style so your problem is more difficult. Many old houses now being remodeled are tall and narrow. For them planting must mitigate height and give a down-to-the-ground effect. This can be accomplished with low-growing trees—Arnold crabapple, Christmas-berry, or Siebold viburnum —placed at the corners of the house. Between them in a staggered row, you might plant one kind of shrub. For a tall house a good combination with the trees would be inkberry or Japanese holly and myrtle for groundcover.

The ranch house usually requires plants that will not exceed 3 feet at maturity. Here one or more low-growing evergreens will suffice as boxleaf holly, dwarf andromeda or low yews. Remember that windows have been placed to give light and air or to frame a view so avoid defeating this purpose by planting shrubs in front that will grow tall. For the salt-box type, a maple tree, placed at a little distance, will provide a suitable frame. If the foundation wall is attractive, then planting is not necessary. I think of one old Connecticut farmhouse where the foundation stones are so beautiful that all we planted was a groundcover of myrtle. A contemporary house may require only a low hedge of holly, a clump of shadbush to soften corners, or a groundcover below the windows.

Natural and unnatural surroundings

How to relate your planting to the site comes next. A house on a hill needs horizontal rather than upright plants, junipers or creeping roses that stand wind. In a low open field a house is often well set off by upright growers, perhaps a few trees planted at the rear to form a background. In a woodland it is wise to use the type of plants that would naturally grow there. Always make the planting appropriate to conditions whether your house is at the edge of the Arizona desert, on a rocky ledge in Maine, or

3. The Approach to the House

on an old plantation in the South. And if your house faces northeast, be sure to select plants that can survive lack of sun.

When an unhealthy condition is caused by dripping water from an overhang, don't try to grow plants directly below for they will not live long. Instead I suggest using brick or gravel to extend 1 to 2 feet out from the foundation of the house. This will provide adequate surface drainage and you can then safely plant there beyond the danger zone.

Characteristics of plants

Plants that have a good year-round appearance and are suited to your climate and soil are the ones for you to choose. Limit yourself to perhaps not more than three kinds. They must be hardy, long-lived, increasing in beauty and interest with the years. This does not mean that all must be evergreen for you will also enjoy deciduous flowering shrubs; but whatever is chosen should be in scale with your house. If this is quite small, inkberry, creeping juniper, rockspray cotoneaster, or bayberry will look well. And for a Cape Cod house, my favorites are sweet-fern, *Comptonia asplenifolia,* with this, common bayberry, which may need a yearly clipping to keep it in bounds.

The color of flowers in relation to the color of your house is a consideration. If yours is red brick, white dogwoods will look far better than pink. With a gray shingled house, pink dogwood would be charming or some of the azaleas in shades of pink or yellow.

Here is a limited list of small trees and shrubs to plant around your house. As you select be sure you know the color, height at maturity and possible spread of each plant.

Small Trees

Amelanchier canadensis	Shadbush or serviceberry
Betula papyrifera	Paper birch; tall grower
pendula alba	White birch (single or clump)
populifolia	Gray birch (clumps, subject to miner)
Cornus florida	Flowering dogwood
Kousa chinensis	Chinese dogwood
mas	Cornelian-cherry
Crataegus Oxycantha	English hawthorn or May-tree
Phaenopyrum	Washington thorn
Halesia carolina	Silverbell
Juniperus virginiana	Red-cedar
Laburnum Vossii	Goldenchain tree
Magnolia stellata	Star magnolia
Malus floribunda Arnoldiana	Arnold crabapple
Photinia villosa	Christmas-berry
Tsuga canadensis	Canada hemlock

Shrubs

Abelia grandiflora	Glossy abelia
Azalea, selected forms	
Cotoneaster horizontalis	Rockspray cotoneaster
Ilex crenata	Japanese holly
convexa	Boxleaf holly
microphylla	Littleleaf holly
glabra	Inkberry or winterberry
Juniperus, selected forms	Juniper
Kalmia latifolia	Mountain-laurel
Leucothoe axillaris	Dwarf leucothoe
Catesbaei	Drooping leucothoe
Myrica pensylvanica	Bayberry
Pieris floribunda	Dwarf andromeda
japonica	Japanese andromeda
Rhododendron carolinianum	Carolina rhododendron
Taxus, selected forms	Yew
Vaccinium corymbosum	Highbush blueberry
Viburnum Carlesii	Fragrant viburnum
Lentago	Nannyberry
Sieboldii	Siebold viburnum
tomentosum	Doublefile viburnum

15

Approach
for a
front door
above
a drive

Trees

Cornus florida	Flowering dogwood
Halesia carolina	Silverbell-tree
Malus 'Red Jade'	Weeping crabapple
Quercus palustris	Pin oak
Sophora japonica	Japanese pagoda-tree

Shrubs

Juniperus chinensis Pfitzeriana	Pfitzer juniper
Sargentii	Sargent juniper
Taxus cuspidata nana	Dwarf Japanese yew

Vines and groundcovers

Hydrangea petiolaris	Climbing hydrangea
Vinca minor	Myrtle or periwinkle

Pot plants

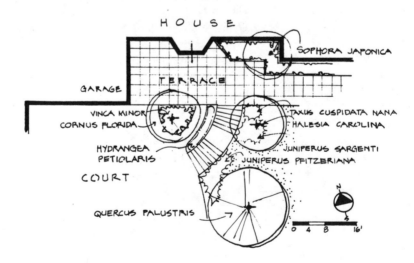

16

The approach to this front-door entrance, some 8 feet above the driveway, required an easy flight of steps with planting for year-round interest. At the left, so as not to conceal the entrance, the dogwood tree is kept pruned to just about the height of the wrought-iron railing. The climbing hydrangea, an excellent though slow-growing vine, is planted at the level of the lowest step and trained gracefully up along the steps and over the door to the basement. At the right, the silverbell-tree, selected for fast growth but medium size in maturity, always looks attractive. At the top of the steps Sargent juniper stays low while Pfitzer juniper billows out below, giving needed height along the drive. Both evergreens have fine winter color. Potted plants of African lily, *Agapanthus umbellatus,* 'Red Jade' crabapple, and late chrysanthemums bring summer and autumn color to this informal approach.

17

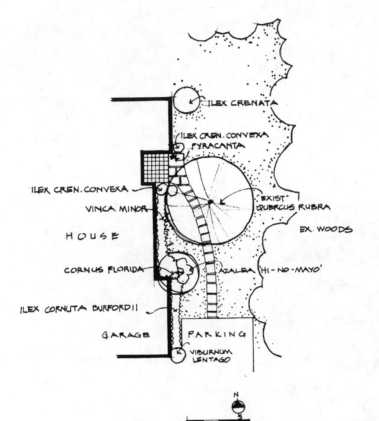

Tree
    Cornus florida   Flowering dogwood

Shrubs
    Azalea 'Hi-no-mayo'   Pink azalea
    Ilex cornuta Burfordii   Burford holly
        crenata   Japanese holly
               convexa   Boxleaf holly
    Pyracantha coccinea Lalandii   Firethorn
    Viburnum Lentago   Nannyberry

Groundcover
    Vinca minor   Myrtle or periwinkle

18

Planting for a concealed front door

When the front door is hidden from immediate view, a path and planting are the only means of indicating the main entrance. Here the curved path, both directional and inviting, and an asymmetrical placement of low hollies, accented by an espaliered pyracantha, show the way to the door in the alcove. A white dogwood breaks the long line of the house with pink azaleas and purple and white myrtle below for a colorful ground planting. This low extended house required a planting that would stay in scale and be of year-round interest.

This hospitable entrance of Helen Van Pelt Wilson's house in Connecticut is framed by a fringe-tree selected for its multiple stems and drooping panicles of fragrant white flowers in early June followed in fall by bright yellow foliage. The tree is pruned to keep trunks clean of foliage and the top spreading but fairly open so that sunlight sifts through to house plants summering on the steps and on the broad stone platform. Myrtle with early bulbs and later lilies bring more fragrance to this doorway where there is special interest in scented plants. Fragrant plants are carried around the corner along the walk to the driveway and include French hybrid lilacs, winter honeysuckle, and fragrant viburnum.

BRADBURY PHOTO

Planting for a front door and garden entrance

Trees

Betula pendula alba	White birch
Chionanthus virginica	Fringe-tree

Shrubs

Lonicera fragrantissima	Winter honeysuckle
Photinia villosa	Christmas-berry
Syringa Lemoinei	French hybrid lilac
Viburnum Carlesii	Fragrant viburnum

Groundcover

Vinca minor	Myrtle or periwinkle

Bulbs

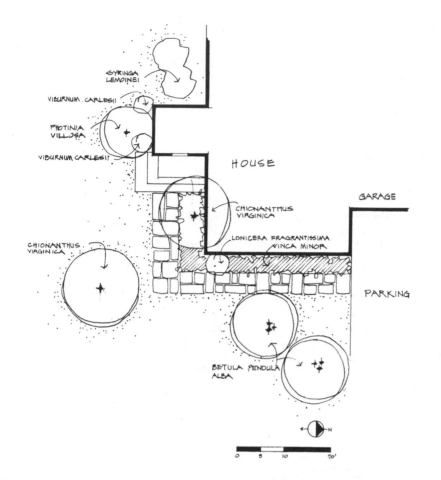

SYRINGA LEMOINEI

VIBURNUM CARLESII

PHOTINIA VILLOSA

VIBURNUM CARLESII

HOUSE

GARAGE

CHIONANTHUS VIRGINICA

LONICERA FRAGRANTISSIMA
VINCA MINOR

CHIONANTHUS VIRGINICA

PARKING

BETULA PENDULA ALBA

S ● N

0   5   10   20'

Here is the fringe-tree in bloom, and around the corner the Christmas-berry shades the plant-room in summer and lilacs bring more fragrance. MINER PHOTO, courtesy *Home Garden*

Trees

Cornus florida	Flowering dogwood
Malus	Apple
Quercus palustris	Pin oak
Ulmus americana	American elm

Shrubs

Azalea 'Delaware Valley White'	
nudiflora	Pinxterbloom
'Palestrina'	White
Vaseyi	Pinkshell
Ilex crenata	Japanese holly
rotundifolia	Roundleaf holly
Kalmia latifolia	Mountain-laurel
Pieris japonica	Japanese andromeda
Taxus cuspidata nana	Dwarf yew

Groundcover

Vinca minor	Myrtle or periwinkle

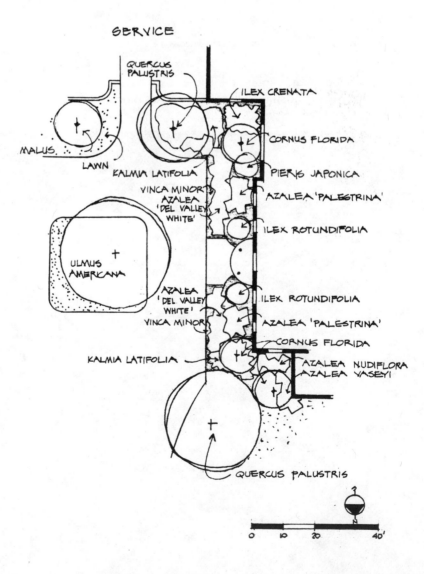

This Georgian house built in the center of an open field needed trees to frame it and other plants to soften the formality of the entrance. Pin oaks and dogwoods provide a charming setting, azaleas give bloom, mountain-laurel and Japanese andromeda year-round green with the groundcover of myrtle. Low white azaleas make a front planting that is colorful in spring and attractive through the rest of the year. The roundleaf hollies at each side of the front door are of naturally globular form and trimmed to look like the more tender box.

Planting for a Georgian house

Planting
around a
Cape Cod house

A Cape Cod house on a long narrow lot at the end of a lane needed a flowering tree to soften the sharp corner of the garage and carry the eye to the front door. Here we planted a flowering dogwood, which has good form and gray buds in winter, beautiful spring flowers, and stunning fall color. Behind the low wall the boxleaf holly with groundcover of blue bugleweed makes the small entrance area easy to maintain. Dwarf yews at each side of the door set off the wide porch steps and stay in scale.

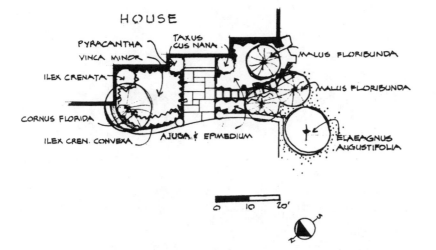

Trees

    Cornus florida   Flowering dogwood
    Elaeagnus augustifolia   Russian olive
    Malus floribunda   Showy crabapple

Shrubs

    Ilex crenata   Japanese holly
              convexa   Boxleaf holly
    Pyracantha coccinea Lalandii   Firethorn
    Taxus cuspidata nana   Dwarf yew

Groundcovers

    Ajuga reptans   Bugleweed
    Epimedium grandiflorum niveum Snowy epimedium
    Vinca minor   Myrtle or periwinkle

25

Planting
for a
modified
Regency house

Trees

Betula populifolia   Gray birch
Cornus florida   Flowering dogwood

Shrubs

Ilex Aquifolium   English holly
    crenata   Japanese holly
Rhododendron 'Boule de Neige'   Dwarf white
Taxus cuspidata Thayerae   Spreading Japanese yew

Vines and Groundcovers

Hedera Helix   English ivy
Vinca minor   Myrtle or periwinkle

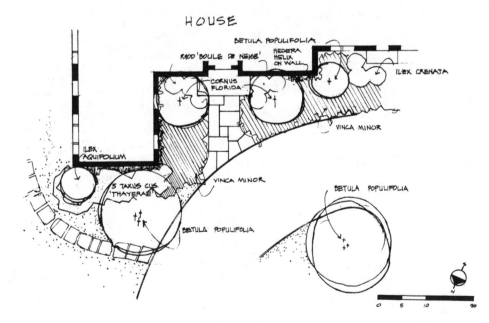

To frame this Regency entrance, a pair of flowering dogwoods were selected since these are attractive in every season. A few low rhododendrons, 'Boule de Neige', offer white flowers in early summer and good evergreen foliage for winter, all in a groundcover of myrtle. English ivy climbing over white brick walls is trimmed to emphasize the doorway; the service entrance at the right is shielded with Japanese holly and a clump of gray birch.

27

4.

Terrace Plantings

Terraces offer delightful opportunity for outdoor living and dining, places to read and rest or just to sit and dream. You may want one large terrace close to the house for entertaining, another smaller secluded one yards away where you can enjoy being alone to read or have a cup of tea, perhaps a third for sunning and a view of the baby's playpen. The needs of your family, the surrounding land, and the neighborhood dictate in large measure what you can do to develop agreeable living rooms outdoors.

Guide lines

Terraces can be developed in various ways but easy access from the house is a necessity. Need for privacy will help you decide whether to plant a low hedge or a high wall of evergreens. Prevailing winds are to be considered. A corner, perhaps between wings of the house, may be nicely sheltered but too enclosed for summer use. Above all, a terrace should look out on something—a view of mountains or oceans, a garden of your own making, or perhaps just one venerable tree.

If the place for your terrace is not flat, considerable grading may be necessary to make it so or to provide several levels for an interesting series of terraces. Then wide steps with low risers will make it easy to move from one level to another. Perhaps you would like a "sitting wall" to accommodate extra guests or as a place for summering house plants. A sitting wall always gives an outdoor room a nice feeling of enclosure. If you want flower beds on your terrace, why not raise them 18 inches to make cultivation effortless.

You can make the floor of brick, flagstone, concrete, grass, or a combination of two materials, as brick and flagstone. Whether you lay these dry in sand and cinders or on a bed of cement, be sure to set with a slight pitch away from the house, a quarter inch per foot, so that water will run off quickly. Much of the success of outdoor entertaining depends on whether a terrace has been constructed so that it is comfortable, above all dry and pleasant to walk on.

The open space beyond the terrace can be developed into a formal or informal garden, or planted with trees and shrubs to provide a pleasant vista. However you plan, keep in mind that house, terrace, and the open areas adjacent are closely related and that a terrace can be the important link, the graceful transition, between your house and what lies beyond.

You may want to include a feature—birdbath or bird feeder or a pool and a little fountain with a re-circulating pump. The sound of dripping water is delightful in hot weather.

Plants for the terrace

When it comes to planting, first consider a tree, a kind you like, and the place it will go. Shade is essential and the pattern of shifting light and shadow cool and restful in the heat; in winter the bare branches of a great tree against a bleak sky are beautiful to dwell upon particularly after a light fall of snow. Consider a pin oak or red maple if you need a big tree; a flowering tree if something smaller will do, perhaps with double or multiple trunks—a dogwood, magnolia, silverbell, shadbush, or fringe-tree. These have lovely blossoms in April, May, or June and all develop interesting outlines.

You will want some evergreens too. A low hedge of holly, yew, or pachistima will stay in bounds below windows and always look neat and attractive. Or you may need a tall evergreen for a windbreak; a white pine grows quickly and develops a handsome form. Against the house wall, an espaliered pyracantha would be attractive with spring blossoms and red-orange autumn berries that the birds love.

There are many beautiful shrubs to plant near a summer terrace—the low *Abelia grandiflora,* which blooms for three months or more, or *Caryopteris* 'Heavenly Blue' with color through most of July. For shade there are the newer dwarf rhododendrons 'Ramapo' or 'Windbeam' that flower in May. If your house is small, a lilac or the fragrant viburnum at the corner will look just right.

Every terrace needs some color. Potted plants—geraniums, lantanas, begonias, fuchsias, impatiens, heliotrope—offer all-summer bloom. Group pots at the edge of steps, beside the door, even on the sitting wall. So many annuals and tender perennials flourish in containers either in sun or shade that you can work out any color scheme you want.

These pictures and plans show terraces planned for families with special needs and interests. Because each terrace was well thought out from the beginning, it became an attractive, satisfactory place for outdoor living. You can get ideas here to help you design a terrace that will be just right for you.

Summary

Plan adequate terraces for outdoor living with walls, fences, or hedges for seclusion and protection from wind.

Design with something to look at—a view of ocean, countryside, or garden of your own making.

Provide a proper terrace floor, paving or grass; always with ease of maintenance in mind.

Include a feature for special interest.

Select a tree for summer shade, some evergreens for winter effect, and flowering plants for summer color.

Use containers wherever possible.

Tree
    Cornus florida   Flowering dogwood

Shrubs
    Ilex crenata   Japanese holly
    Taxus cuspidata capitata   Upright yew

Groundcover
    Pachysandra terminalis   Pachysandra

Terrace under tall trees

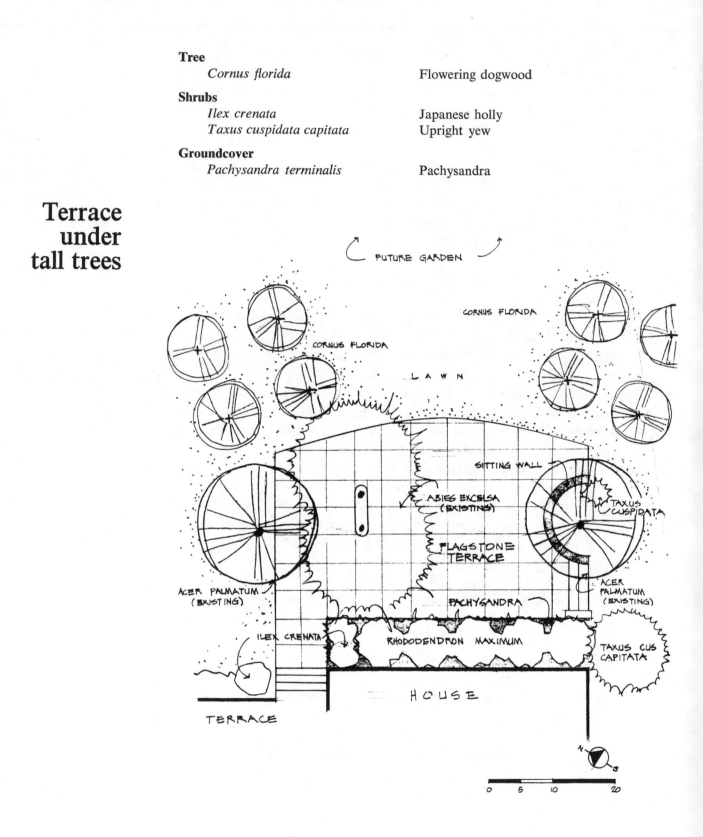

30

A spacious terrace under trees accommodates a family with many children and their friends who enjoy dining and sitting in this shaded place with flowering dogwoods close by in the field. The terrace and wall were designed around two groups of existing trees. One of the Japanese maples is seen behind the wall with an upright yew below; two tall spruces are included in the paving. It is worth noting that trees are not injured if a terrace is laid without mortar and with ample space left around trunks. Since the flagstones are level with the lawn, it is easy to extend entertaining onto the grass, and the low wall around the Japanese maple provides extra sitting space. To give an interesting view throughout the year, a green garden is now being planned in an open field adjacent to the terrace.

Where ground slopes sharply away from the house, a deck may be better than a terrace and serve the same purpose. Here low Andorra junipers at the corners relate deck to lawn, spreading out and softening the stark overhang. At the corner of the house a clump of fragrant viburnums makes a pleasing accent. A thick layer of gravel is wisely spread under the deck to preclude the growth of weeds there. Clara Coffey, L.A.

Juniperus horizontalis plumosa   Plume or Andorra juniper
Viburnum Carlesii   Fragrant viburnum

Planting below a deck

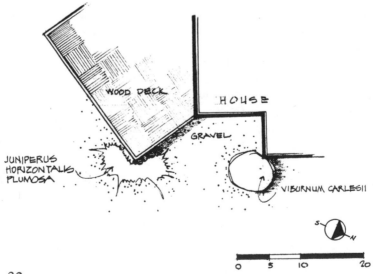

JUNIPERUS HORIZONTALIS PLUMOSA

WOOD DECK

HOUSE

GRAVEL

VIBURNUM CARLESII

0   5   10   20

A 12 x 15-foot terrace planned for two occupies a sunny place outside a dining room and is delightful for early spring and late fall dining. Since it is placed well above the driveway below, this terrace affords a view of a green garden beyond. On one side protection from the street was assured by an existing planting of tall yews. To conceal the service entrance on the other side, a 6-foot brick wall was built, and this also makes a background for a small pool with a tiny fountain that brings the cool sound of dripping water. A false-cypress, not shown in this view, makes a nice corner accent. A clematis with single white flowers climbs gracefully over the wall at the end of the pool, and potted geraniums make colorful accents.

Trees

Chamaecyparis obtusa nana Hinoki false-cypress
Cornus Kousa chinensis Chinese dogwood

Shrubs

Forsythia intermedia Border forsythia
Ilex cornuta rotunda Dwarf Chinese holly

Vine

Clematis Henryi Large-flowered white

Herbs

Terrace for two

Trees
    Cornus Kousa chinensis   Chinese dogwood
    Tsuga canadensis   Canada hemlock

Shrubs
    Leucothoe Catesbaei   Drooping leucothoe
    Taxus media Hatfieldii   Hedge yew

Vines and groundcovers
    Clematis paniculata   Sweet autumn clematis
    Rosa 'Golden Showers'   Yellow climbing rose
    Vinca minor   Myrtle or periwinkle
    Wisteria sinensis   Chinese wisteria

        Bulbs, perennials, roses, bedding plants

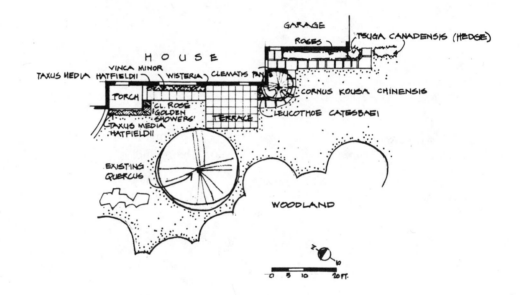

34

Beside this Cape Cod house in a woodland setting, a small flagstone terrace, level with the lawn, was designed for easy outdoor living. It is adjacent to the dining room and a wide path connects it with the small porch so that the two are well related. The properly graded lawn is about 25 feet wide and reaches from the terrace to the woods beyond. A multiple-stemmed Chinese dogwood at the corner, with drooping leucothoe below, protects the terrace from a service walk. A yellow rose climbs up a porch pillar which is surrounded by a hedge of upright hedge yews. A purple wisteria makes a charming frame for the large window and also shades the living room in summer. In the narrow bed below, a little garden has recently been planted with spring bulbs including white tulips, interplanted with blue forget-me-nots, *Myosotis semperflorens,* followed by yellow Marguerites, *Chrysanthemum frutescens,* which bloom all summer. BUHLE PHOTO

Terrace level with the lawn

35

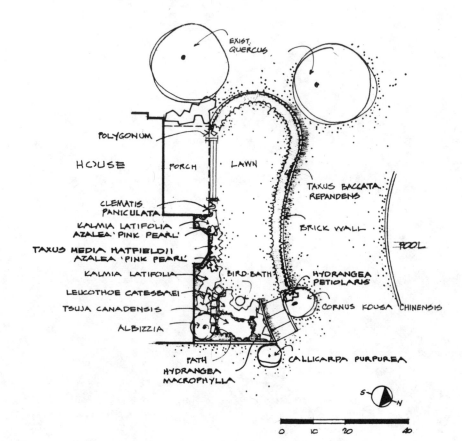

Trees

Albizzia Julibrissin	Silk-tree
Cornus Kousa chinensis	Chinese dogwood
Tsuga canadensis	Canada hemlock

Shrubs

Azalea 'Pink Pearl'	
Callicarpa purpurea	Beautyberry
Hydrangea macrophylla	Blue hydrangea
Kalmia latifolia	Mountain-laurel
Leucothoe Catesbaei	Drooping leucothoe
Taxus baccata repandens	Spreading English yew
media Hatfieldii	Hedge yew

Vines

Clematis paniculata	Sweet autumn clematis
Hydrangea paniculata	Climbing hydrangea
Polygonum Aubertii	Silver-lace or fleece-vine

36

A porch and grass terrace

Here a terrace becomes a transition from the open porch of a country house to the inviting wide step-ramp of brick that leads to a pool terrace below. The retaining wall, also of brick, is outlined with spreading English yews. Sweet autumn clematis clambers over the porch roof and 'Pink Pearl' azaleas look lovely with clumps of laurel under the bay window. A birdbath at the end of the terrace is surrounded with drooping leucothoe and blue hydrangeas for summer bloom. Coming down the ramp to the pool, you notice a fine Chinese dogwood growing at the corner.

A large
terrace
for
summer use

Trees

Acer rubrum	Red maple
Betula populifolia	Gray birch
Cornus florida	Flowering dogwood
Juniperus virginiana	Red-cedar
Malus 'Red Jade'	Weeping crabapple

Shrubs

Deutzia gracilis	Slender deutzia
Ilex crenata convexa	Boxleaf holly
Pinus Mugo Mughus	Mugho pine

Annuals, bulbs, bedding plants

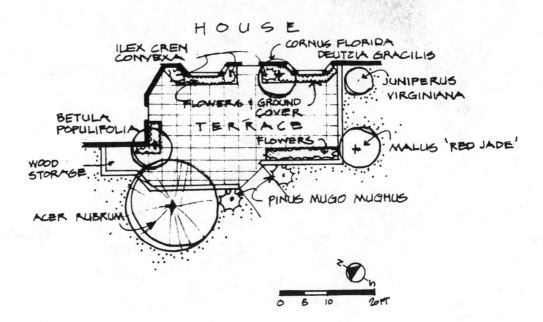

38

A large living terrace planned for summers at home, overlooks a lake in the Connecticut hills and varies in width as it extends across the facade of this remodeled farmhouse. A low wall gives protection from the steep bank. Near the sitting area a red maple, transplanted from nearby woods, gives just the right amount of shade. A clump of gray birch softens the corner and conceals a stack of firewood beyond. Opposite the dining-room windows against a low wall is a narrow border bright in spring with pink tulips 'Clara Butt' and white tulips 'Mt. Tacoma,' the edging of purple pansies. Later the same color scheme is carried out with pink and white lantanas and sweet alyssum.

39

A sunny brick terrace

Trees
- *Ilex opaca* — American holly
- *Juniperus virginiana* — Red-cedar
- *Liriodendron Tulipifera* — Tulip-tree

Shrubs
- *Ilex cornuta Burfordii* — Burford holly
- *crenata convexa* — Boxleaf holly
- *Leucothoe Catesbaei* — Drooping leucothoe
- *Syringa vulgaris alba* — Common white lilac

Vines
- *Clematis paniculata* — Sweet autumn clematis
- *Jasminum nudiflorum* — Winter jasmine

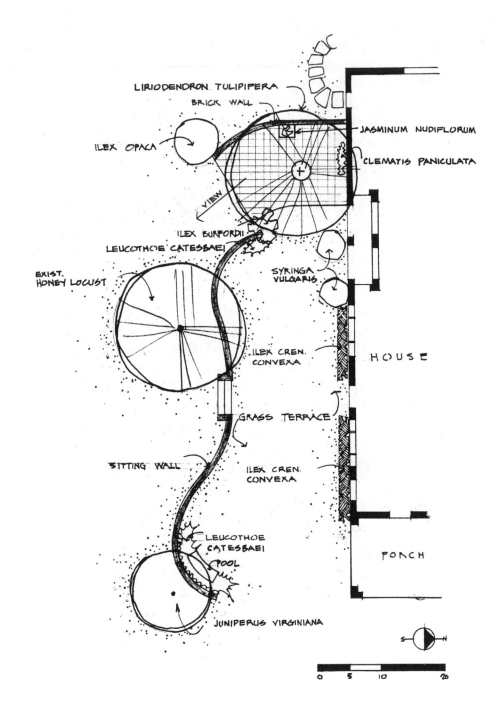

LIRIODENDRON TULIPIFERA

BRICK WALL

ILEX OPACA

JASMINUM NUDIFLORUM

CLEMATIS PANICULATA

VIEW

ILEX BURFORDII

LEUCOTHOE CATESBAEI

EXIST.
HONEY LOCUST

SYRINGA
VULGARIS

ILEX CREN.
CONVEXA

HOUSE

GRASS TERRACE

SITTING WALL

ILEX CREN.
CONVEXA

LEUCOTHOE
CATESBAEI

POOL

PORCH

JUNIPERUS VIRGINIANA

S · N

0   5   10   20

A 5-foot brick wall conceals vegetable garden and compost pile and gives an enclosed feeling to this small brick terrace, which serves also as a sun-trap in winter. The tulip-tree in the center provides summer shade both to terrace and upstairs window. Sweet autumn clematis and winter jasmine will eventually make nice patterns on the wall. The adjacent grass terrace has a low sitting wall and both terraces offer lovely views of the nearby marshland and water.

41

5.
Trees and Their Associations

Trees are the strongest structural element in your plan so it is important to select just the right ones and then to place them properly. However, if you have a house in woodland, thinning out may be all that is required, or the answer may lie not in new specimens but in high pruning of old ones for a restful cathedral-like feeling. Just one fine tree can set the scale for all your other planting but sometimes there is not even one tree to start with, particularly in developments where contractors may have indiscriminately leveled everything to the ground. On a small plot that we designed in the midst of a 100-acre hay field there was not a single tree so we had to plant for immediate shade. We selected a plane-tree, pin oaks, and several flowering crabapples and hawthorns—all fairly fast growing.

As you learn to recognize trees, you will find them a never-ending source of pleasure. Driving along a parkway in winter, you will be aware of the variety of forms, the pin oak with horizontal branches, the honey-locust stretching out to catch the winter light, the severely upright poplars, the graceful weeping willow, a cloud of gold from January on. Do discover the wide-spreading hawthorns with their bright red berries and the stratified sassafras growing in thickets and along the edge of the road.

As you read on and study the planting plans, you will notice that dogwoods have been used over and over for they are most versatile. Form and color are excellent in every season and they seem to suit every situation except perhaps a windy corner. A city-dweller, I have even learned to like our ailanthus trees. After a snowstorm each tall trunk and stiff awkward branch looks as if it had been carefully painted in white stripes. Although ailanthus do leaf out rather late in spring, they make a pleasant summer canopy for our tiny garden.

Selection of trees

When you are thinking about trees for your place, try to answer these questions. What is their function here? Are they for a background or to frame the house? Do we want shade for the terrace or shadows on the lawn? Will grass grow under them? Are deciduous or evergreen trees more appropriate or do we need both? (Every year as the leaves fall, you will realize afresh the importance of evergreens.) What trees will be in good scale and fit well into our plan? Which trees will thrive here?

Keep referring to your plan. It plainly shows the important aspects of your house and grounds—how large the open area is, where shade or screen is needed. It may also indicate a telegraph pole you want to block out or a busy road to be concealed.

Before you buy a tree, be sure you know how large it will eventually grow, what form it will take—upright like the Lombardy poplar or cedar, oval like the sugar maple, drooping like the willow. Do you want a single or multiple-stemmed specimen? Young plants in the nursery rarely have the shape they will develop in five to ten years. A small Chinese dogwood is as awkward as an adolescent but in maturity it has a lovely form. Consider texture and color of foliage in summer and also in fall. Can you look forward to rich autumn hues? Think about how trees look in winter. Some have very interesting structures and color then, as the gray-trunked magnolias and the white birches.

Evergreens, usually slow growing and therefore longer in maturing, are essential for their good green winter color, their forms, their attraction for birds, and particularly for the character they give to a planting. Conifers offer the strongest and darkest effect. When you buy young trees, branches will be full to the ground but, if you have old pines or spruces, you know how clear the trunks stand and how high the branches are above your head. White pines normally grow faster than other evergreens and so are useful when quick screening is needed.

Spacing and root system

Do set out your trees so that there is room for them to develop without crowding. A 75 x 150-foot lot can accommodate but one shade tree and only two or three smaller flowering kinds. Plant the major trees with at least 30 feet between them, the smaller ones 15 feet apart. Too many trees soon crowd a small property. But perhaps you want to create a woodland; then you can follow nature's example and plant trees quite close together, and this is also right for a formal allée.

The type of root system, whether tap or fibrous, makes a difference in spacing and also in opportunity for planting underneath. Willows, Norway maples, and poplars have greedy roots close to the surface. Avoid these for lawn areas. Select instead for a large tree one of the oaks; their roots go deep into the soil and ericaceous plants—azaleas, rhododendrons, and huckleberries—grow well under them. Perennial gardens can be developed under apple trees with beautiful spring pictures when the trees are in blossom and the early perennials bloom beneath them. Birch and crabapple are two deep-rooted smaller trees for lawns and gardens.

Guide to tree selection

Choose deciduous trees in good scale for your property and before you buy, find out about their color, texture, and mature form.

Plant evergreens as space permits.

Check the type of root system so you may know what under-planting is possible.

Select at the nursery if at all possible and tag the best side of each tree so it can be planted to advantage on your property.

Setting for a handsome evergreen

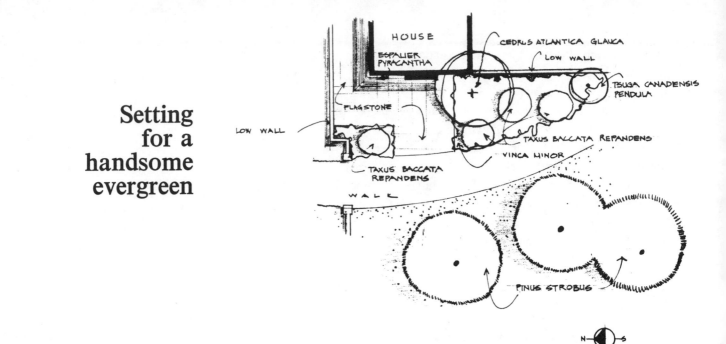

HOUSE

CEDRUS ATLANTICA GLAUCA

ESPALIER PYRACANTHA

LOW WALL

FLAGSTONE

TSUGA CANADENSIS PENDULA

LOW WALL

TAXUS BACCATA REPANDENS

VINCA MINOR

TAXUS BACCATA REPANDENS

WALL

PINUS STROBUS

N S

0 5 10 20

Framed between the clean lofty trunks of two white pines is a magnificent blue Atlas cedar, *Cedrus atlantica glauca,* filling the corner of the house, an unusual climax to the hillside planting and wide terrace path. Although already sizable, it was moved here from a previous home and has grown well, always watered deeply through summer. The needlelike foliage is soft to touch and the tiny cones appearing early in fall stand upright on the branches like little candles.

The honey-locust, *Gleditsia triacanthos,* a large-scale tree suited to this Georgian
house, forms a canopy for the terrace. A fast grower, it makes a splendid summer
showing when the compound leaves let through just the right amount of light for
comfort on the terrace. In winter the long brown pods are interesting. (Also excellent is the thornless 'Moraine' locust which is conveniently non-fruiting; there are
also a number of newer cultivars.) Notice how the triple stems of the dogwood at
the corner of the sun-room are a point of interest there. Pyracantha, trained up a
corner, and clipped Japanese yews, *Taxus cuspidata nana,* complete a restrained
and pleasant planting.

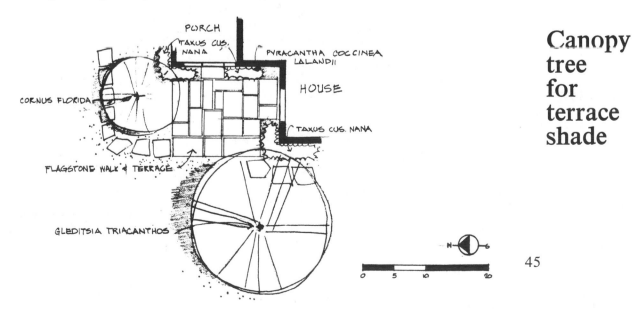

PORCH
TAXUS CUS. NANA
PYRACANTHA COCCINEA LALANDII
HOUSE
CORNUS FLORIDA
TAXUS CUS. NANA
FLAGSTONE WALK & TERRACE
GLEDITSIA TRIACANTHOS

N

0 5 10 20

Canopy
tree
for
terrace
shade

45

The fast-growing goldenrain-tree, *Koelreuteria paniculata,* was planted here to provide quick shade for the south side of this house. It bears large clusters of lovely yellow flowers followed by brown pods that hang on into the fall. The attractive branch structure is a further asset, and this tree is readily propagated from seeds. Small plants of dwarf English box, *Boxus sempervirens suffruticosa,* will soon make a low hedge.

Summer-flowering tree

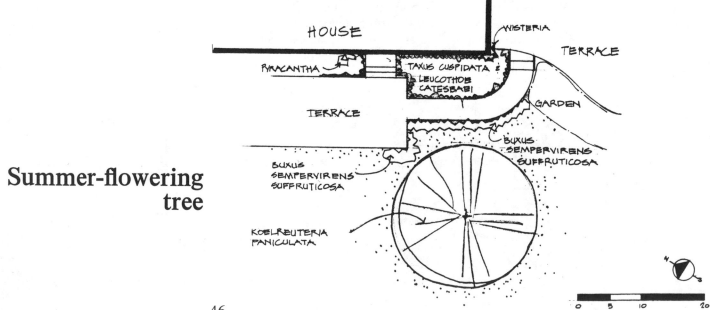

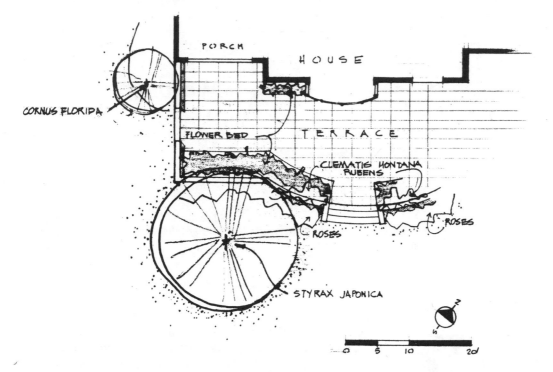

CORNUS FLORIDA · PORCH · HOUSE · FLOWER BED · TERRACE · CLEMATIS MONTANA RUBENS · ROSES · ROSES · STYRAX JAPONICA

0 5 10 20

This old specimen of an unusual flowering tree was moved to this site near the terrace. It gives some shade but its light feathery foliage allows enough sun to come through for the roses below. The Japanese snowbell-tree *Styrax japonica,* with pendulous white bell-shaped flowers in early July is one of my favorite trees.

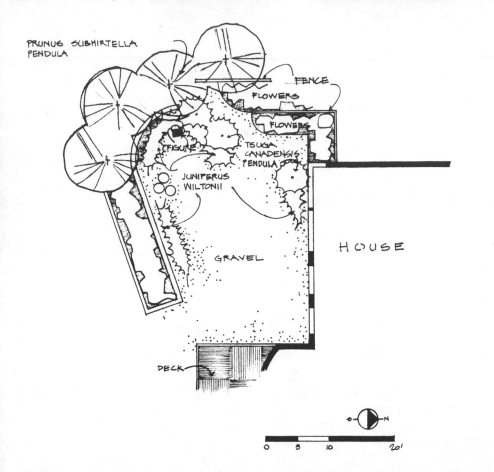

PRUNUS SUBHIRTELLA
PENDULA

FENCE

FLOWERS

FLOWERS

FIGURE

TSUGA
CANADENSIS
PENDULA

JUNIPERUS
WILTONII

GRAVEL

HOUSE

DECK

N

0   5   10   20'

Weeping tree

Trees of drooping habit are often difficult to work into a landscape composition but here two weeping rosebud cherries, *Prunus subhirtella pendula,* are placed to make an attractive setting for a Chinese sculpture. Smaller weeping forms of hemlock, *Tsuga canadensis pendula,* repeat the large shapes while low junipers relate the composition to the ground. A blend of black, white, and pink gravel gives lovely color to this terrace. Clara Coffey, L. A.

Tree with multiple stems to shade a window

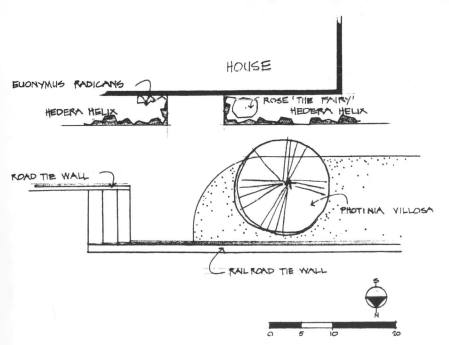

HOUSE

EUONYMUS RADICANS

HEDERA HELIX

ROSE 'THE FAIRY'
HEDERA HELIX

ROAD TIE WALL

PHOTINIA VILLOSA

RAIL ROAD TIE WALL

0   5   10   20

The Christmas-berry, *Photinia villosa,* selected for its multiple stems, is a vigorous grower and soon shaded the wide west windows of this low contemporary house. White flowers in May are followed by red berries—an attraction for the birds—and the leaves turn amber in fall. Eloise A. Ray, L.A.

49

Evergreen and deciduous materials are used together—the sugar maple, *Acer saccharum,* selected for form and color stands at the end of the house; Japanese holly, *Ilex crenata,* by the steps. Beyond the wall the quick-growing Norway spruce, *Abies excelsa* conceals the service area and provides an evergreen frame for the house. In winter the shapely sugar maple has a handsome silhouette as you can see in the other picture.

50

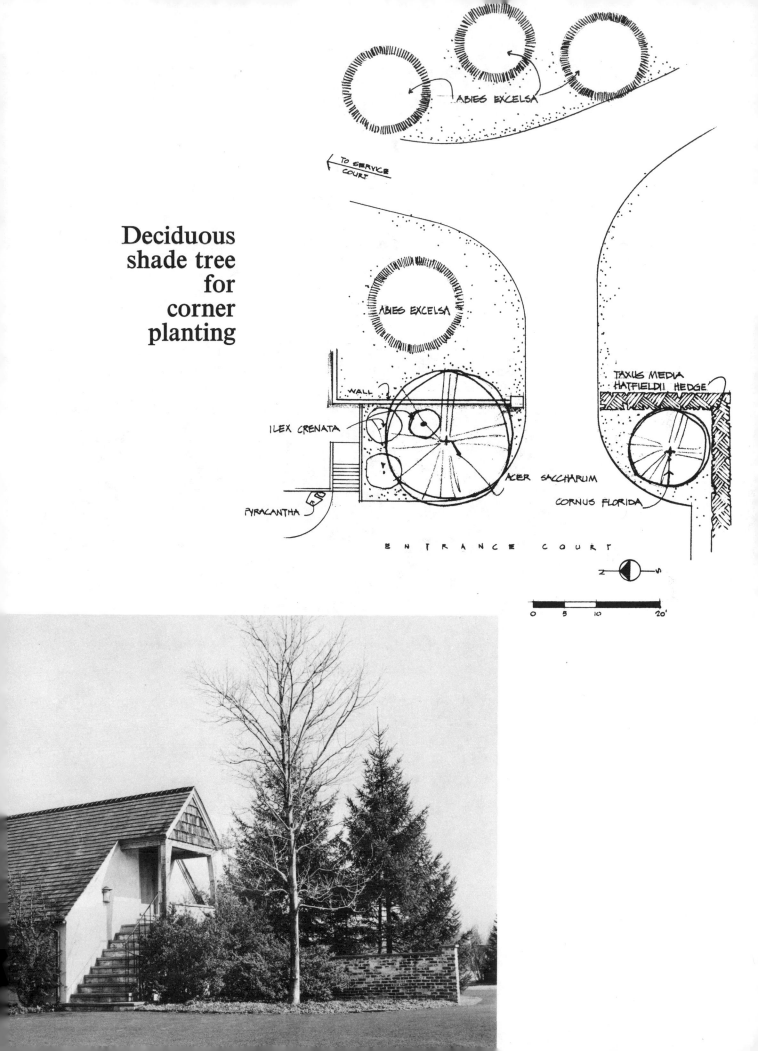

ABIES EXCELSA

TO SERVICE COURT

**Deciduous
shade tree
for
corner
planting**

ABIES EXCELSA

WALL

ILEX CRENATA

TAXUS MEDIA
HATFIELDII HEDGE

PYRACANTHA

ACER SACCHARUM

CORNUS FLORIDA

E N T R A N C E   C O U R T

N — S

0   5   10   20'

Tree with multiple stems for terrace shade

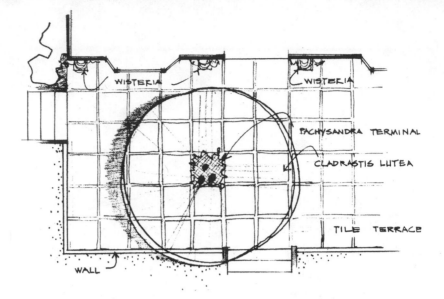

On this large terrace the fast-growing yellowwood, *Cladrastis lutea,* provided almost immediate shade and the double-trunked form makes a dramatic accent. Pendulous clusters of white flowers in June and dense summer foliage are other values.

Native cedar near terrace

This ancient double red-cedar, *Juniperus virginiana,* growing at the bottom of the step-ramp is most effective seen from the end of the house, and the bed of double white petunias contributes to the picture. (Native red-cedars are excellent when you need a narrow tree, for rarely do they branch in this way and they are easily moved in large sizes.)
BUHLE PHOTO

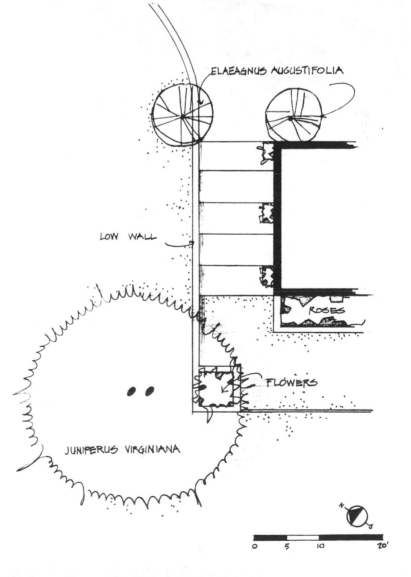

ELAEAGNUS AUGUSTIFOLIA

LOW WALL

ROSES

FLOWERS

JUNIPERUS VIRGINIANA

0   5   10   20'

A spring picture with the white star magnolia 'Water-lily' blooming with white daffodils 'Mt. Hood' on east side of a wall. On the other side, weeping dwarf crabapples, 'Red Jade', are covered with pale pink buds. The flowers are followed by red fruits that hang on through fall and winter. This tree looks well in a garden and here a pair of them accent and continue the long horizontal of the low wall. A tapestry of pansies outlines a bed of roses and iris.

Dwarf flowering tree

54

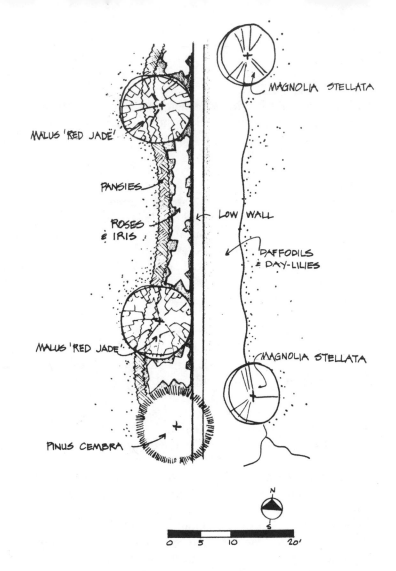

MALUS 'RED JADE'

MAGNOLIA STELLATA

PANSIES

ROSES
& IRIS

LOW WALL

DAFFODILS
& DAY-LILIES

MALUS 'RED JADE'

MAGNOLIA STELLATA

PINUS CEMBRA

N
S

0   5   10   20'

Ten worthwhile major trees

In teaching I have found it helps to consider only a short basic list of trees. From these you can select one or more to meet your needs. Here are my nominations for the most useful major trees, deciduous (D) and evergreen (E):

Botanical Name	Common Name	Growth Rate	Form	Ultimate Height in Feet
Acer rubrum	Red maple D	fast	elliptical	75
saccharum	Sugar maple D	medium	oval	100
Cedrus atlantica glauca	Atlas cedar E	fast	pyramidal	100
Juniperus virginiana	Red-cedar E	fast	columnar	80
Liquidambar Styraciflua	Sweetgum D	fast	pyramidal	100
Pinus nigra	Austrian pine E	fast	pyramidal	90
Strobus	White pine E	fast	rounded	100
Quercus palustris	Pin oak D	fast	pyramidal	75
Tilia cordata	Littleleaf European linden D	slow	pyramidal	90
Tsuga canadensis	Canada hemlock E	medium	pyramidal	90

Twelve fine flowering trees

Botanical Name	Common Name	Growth Rate	Form	Ultimate Height in Feet
Amelanchier canadensis	Shadbush	medium	upright	30
Cornus Kousa chinensis	Chinese dogwood	medium	upright when young	20
Crataegus Crus-galli	Cockspur thorn	fast	rounded	30
Halesia carolina	Silverbell-tree	fast	rounded	30
Koelreuteria paniculata	Goldenrain-tree	fast	rounded	30
Laburnum Vossii	Goldenchain-tree	fast	upright	30
Magnolia Soulangeana	Saucer magnolia	medium	broad	25
Malus floribunda	Showy crabapple		rounded	30
Sargentii	Sargent crabapple		dense low mound	8
Photinia villosa	Christmas-berry		rounded	30
Sophora japonica	Japanese pagoda-tree		rounded	70
Styrax japonica	Japanese snowbell-tree		spreading	30

Natural Associations of Trees and Shrubs

If you are selecting trees and shrubs for a country property or for a woodland setting, perhaps with a stream, observe how some trees group themselves naturally. Do maples, oaks, pines, or junipers predominate in your area? What grows naturally along streams and besides ponds? Here are associations to guide in developing your own plantings.

In Maple Woods
Trees

Acer saccharum	Sugar maple
Betula pendula alba	White birch
Cornus florida	Flowering dogwood
Fagus grandifolia	American beech
Liriodendron Tulipifera	Tulip-tree
Tsuga canadensis	Canada hemlock

Shrubs

Amelanchier oblongifolia	Juneberry
Hamamelis virginiana	Autumn witchhazel
Taxus canadensis	Ground-hemlock
Viburnum acerifolium	Mapleleaf viburnum
Lantana	Wayfaring-tree

In Oak Woods
Trees

Liriodendron Tulipifera	Tulip-tree
Ostrya virginiana	Ironwood
Prunus serotina	Wild black cherry
Quercus alba	White oak
coccinea	Scarlet oak
rubra	Red oak
velutina	Black oak
Sassafras albidum	Sassafras

Shrubs

Azalea nudiflorum	Pinxterbloom
Ilex verticillata	Winterberry
Kalmia latifolia	Mountain-laurel
Vaccinium pensylvanicum	Blueberry

In Pine Woods
Trees

Pinus resinosa	Red pine
rigida	Pitch pine
Strobus	White pine

Few shrubs appear in natural woodland but ferns and wild flowers grow there; wild-flower nurseries now supply these.

Ferns and wild flowers

Cornus canadensis	Bunchberry
Cypripedium acaule	Lady-slipper
Dryopteris marginalis	Shield or wood fern
Gaultheria procumbens	Checkerberry or wintergreen
Mitchella repens	Partridge-berry
Polystichum acrostichoides	Christmas fern
Solidago canadensis	Canada goldenrod

On Juniper Slopes

Trees

Juniperus virginiana	Red-cedar
Robinia Pseudo-Acacia	False acacia (locust)

Shrubs

Cornus racemosa	Gray dogwood
Juniperus communis	Common juniper
Lonicera sempervirens	Trumpet honeysuckle
Myrica caroliniensis	Bayberry
Quercus ilicifolia	Scrub oak
Rhus glabra	Smooth sumac
Rosa blanda	Meadow rose
Vaccinium pensylvanicum	Blueberry
Viburnum dentatum	Arrow-wood
Lentago	Nannyberry
prunifolium	Blackhaw
Zanthoxylum americanum	Prickly-ash

Beside Stream or Pond

Trees

Acer Negundo	Box-elder
rubrum	Red maple
Carpinus caroliniana	American hornbeam
Carya glabra	Pignut
ovata	Shagbark hickory
Celtis occidentalis	Hackberry
Crataegus Crus-galli	Cockspur thorn
Fraxinus americana	White ash
Platanus occidentalis	Buttonwood or sycamore
Populus candicans	Balm-of-Gilead
Quercus palustris	Pin oak
Salix nigra	Black willow

Shrubs

Alnus rugosa	Hazel or smooth alder
Clethra alnifolia	Sweet pepperbush
Hamamelis virginiana	Autumn witchhazel
Lindera aestivale	Spicebush
Salix discolor	Pussywillow
Sambucus canadensis	American or sweet elder

Part II

Which Place Is Yours?

The ten planting plans that follow have all been successfully carried out. I believe they are typical enough for you to find ideas in them for your own place. Although the properties varied greatly and there were specific requirements for each one, there were also basic needs common to all: a pleasing and proper approach, shade trees, screening for privacy, at least one terrace, emphasis on plants of year-round attractiveness, and always a plea for low maintenance.

The number of plants you buy for a given space depends first upon their size in maturity and second upon how soon you wish to have the look of a completed planting. Usually the third year after setting out is the best.

6.
Remodeled Hillside Property

The house is situated in a community of attractive stone dwellings built some years ago in hilly woodland near a city. It is a corner property, 110 x 175 feet. When the house became inadequate for the growing family, an addition was planned and, wisely, a general landscape plan was worked out at the same time to give privacy and to include a gracious new approach, terraces, a place for children to play, and also work areas. The young couple wanted planting that would be attractive and interesting through the year but would require only minimum upkeep. Beech and oak trees towering over the house set the scale.

The wide front ramp was first planned with flagstone treads and brownstone risers but the cost went beyond the budget and railroad ties with wood chips were substituted. Baltic ivy outlines this ramp and covers the slope beneath the spreading beech. The retaining wall by the courtyard repeats the brownstone of the building and is softened by English ivy. Above the garage the proposed wing will be constructed and here the front door will be placed. A Japanese snowbell-tree has already been planted as accent and frame for the new entrance. Looking down over the courtyard from the upper level, you see a brook through clumps of hemlock and white birch. The trees were placed to enclose the courtyard and to block out the view of the house next door. Most of the landscape work was started as soon as the garage was completed, and a number of existing shrubs and evergreens —rhododendron, laurel, and yew—were transplanted to an enbankment near the road and new plants were ordered for the various garden areas.

The dining room, sheltered by an old oak tree, opens onto a large terrace with easy access for serving. The lawn area was raised to conceal the movement of cars on the road below and also to provide a fairly level area adjacent to the terrace. The planting, designed with a vista to lawns beyond, gives the impression of an English park. Around the open lawn dwarf white rhododendrons and azaleas are of year-round interest.

Outside the children's garage-playroom a gravel area is planned for bicycles and play. The larger play space with swings, jungle-gym, and tent is surrounded by a thick hedge of Japanese holly that keeps the youngsters from running into the street.

Behind the house there is a tiny terrace with lawn and a pool, delightful to watch from a kitchen window for the birds visit it constantly. It is surrounded by boxleaf holly. The steep embankment is also terraced. From it steps lead down toward an old apple tree on the neighbor's property, past a hidden terrace, and then below to compost area and courtyard.

A wide step-ramp—more informal than other kinds of steps and better suited to this property—leads up to the proposed new entrance already graced by the beech tree. The groundcover is Baltic ivy, and dwarf yews accent the steps.

PITKIN PHOTO

61

Grading raised the level of the lawn to help conceal the road below. Banks of white and light pink rhododendrons and azaleas give privacy but with an opening for a vista up the slope and through existing trees, as in a park. Shrubs with pale flowers are pleasing for a terrace used most often in the evening. PITKIN PHOTO

Under the shade of a giant oak, the flagstone terrace in the corner of the house insures privacy and a comfortable place for outdoor living. Dwarf yellow and white azaleas give color along the service wing with a sorrel-tree to interrupt the roof line. PITKIN PHOTO

The children's play area is spacious and in view of both terrace and kitchen wing.
PITKIN PHOTO

A tiny shallow pool and fountain—a few drops fall each minute—provide water for birds, and a background of shiny boxleaf holly emphasizes the sparkling freshness of this little scene with its appropriate figure. PITKIN PHOTO

The path from kitchen terrace to work area and courtyard is dominated by an ancient apple tree with gnarled trunk and fascinating branching habit. A hedge of Japanese barberry runs along the property line and myrtle covers the bank.

PITKIN PHOTO

This work area with bins for compost and soil is in constant use. Compost is a valuable addition to the upkeep of any property and easily made. Pile up leaves, grass clippings, and other clean garden refuse into three or four sandwich layers—each one foot of leaves, etc. spread with 2 inches of soil. Keep the top saucer-shaped so water will collect, penetrate the pile, and hasten decay. Turn the pile over every three months or so, and in about a year you will have a fine pile of organic material to use on your garden.

Trees

Betula pendula alba	White birch
Cornus florida	Flowering dogwood
Kousa chinensis	Chinese dogwood
mas	Cornelian-cherry
Halesia carolina	Silverbell-tree
Oxydendrum arboreum	Sourwood
Pinus cembra	Swiss stone pine
Styrax japonica	Japanese snowbell-tree
Tsuga canadensis	Canada hemlock

Shrubs

Azalea 'Daviesi'	White with yellow marking
'Gumpo'	Dwarf white
Knap Hill Hybrids	Yellow and white
'Louise Gable'	Peach
'Narcissiflora'	Yellow
'Polaris'	White
'Rose Greeley'	White
'Snow'	White
viscosum	Swamp azalea
Berberis Thunbergii	Japanese barberry
Enkianthus campanulatus	Redvein enkianthus
Ilex crenata	Japanese holly
convexa	Boxleaf holly
'Green Island'	Green Island holly
rotunda	Roundleaf holly
glabra	Inkberry
Pieris japonica	Japanese andromeda
Rhododendron 'Boule de Neige'	White
carolinianum	Carolina rhododendron
catawbiense alba	Mountain rosebay
'Keiskei'	Dwarf yellow
'Mrs. C. S. Sargent'	Pink
'Windbeam'	Dwarf pale pink
Taxus cuspidata	Japanese yew
nana	Dwarf yew
media Hicksii	Hicks yew
Viburnum Carlesii	Fragrant viburnum
prunifolium	Blackhaw

Vines and groundcovers

Hedera Helix	English Ivy
baltica	Baltic ivy
Vinca minor	Myrtle or periwinkle

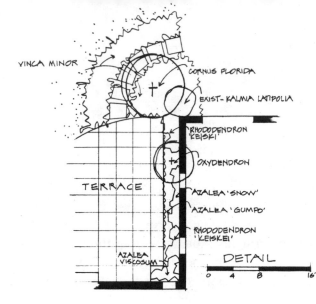

VINCA MINOR

CORNUS FLORIDA

EXIST- KALMIA LATIFOLIA

RHODODENDRON 'KEISKI'

OXYDENDRON

TERRACE

AZALEA 'SNOW'

AZALEA 'GUMPO'

RHODODENDRON 'KEISKEI'

AZALEA VISCOSUM

DETAIL

0 4 8 16'

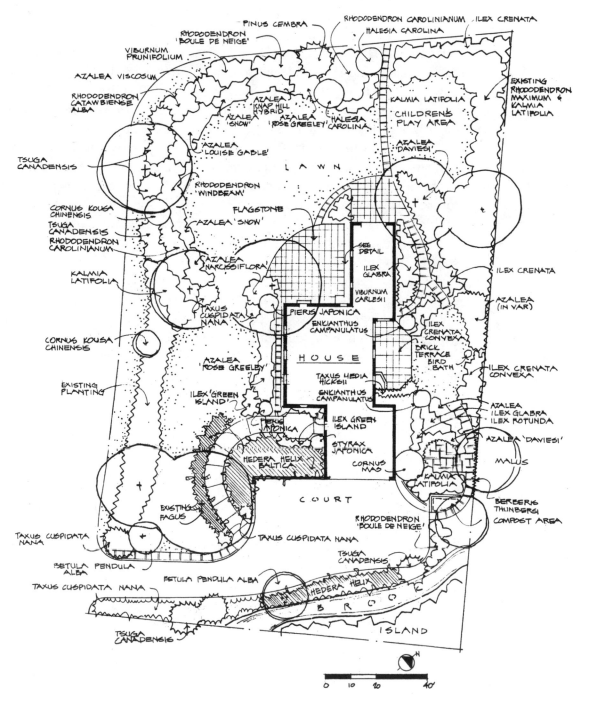

PINUS CEMBRA

RHODODENDRON CAROLINIANUM   ILEX CRENATA

HALESIA CAROLINA

RHODODENDRON 'BOULE DE NEIGE'

VIBURNUM PRUNIFOLIUM

AZALEA VISCOSUM

RHODODENDRON CATAWBIENSE ALBA

AZALEA 'SNOW'

AZALEA KNAP HILL HYBRID

AZALEA 'ROSE GREELEY'

HALESIA CAROLINA

KALMIA LATIFOLIA

CHILDREN'S PLAY AREA

EXISTING RHODODENDRON MAXIMUM & KALMIA LATIFOLIA

AZALEA 'LOUISE GABLE'

AZALEA 'DAVIESI'

TSUGA CANADENSIS

L A W N

RHODODENDRON 'WINDBEAM'

CORNUS KOUSA CHINENSIS

TSUGA CANADENSIS

RHODODENDRON CAROLINIANUM

FLAGSTONE

AZALEA 'SNOW'

SEE DETAIL

ILEX CRENATA

KALMIA LATIFOLIA

AZALEA 'NARCISSIFLORA'

ILEX GLABRA

AZALEA (IN VAR)

VIBURNUM CARLESI

CORNUS KOUSA CHINENSIS

TAXUS CUSPIDATA NANA

PIERIS JAPONICA

ILEX CRENATA CONVEXA

ENKIANTHUS CAMPANULATUS

BRICK TERRACE BIRD BATH

EXISTING PLANTING

AZALEA 'ROSE GREELEY'

H O U S E

ILEX CRENATA CONVEXA

ILEX 'GREEN ISLAND'

TAXUS MEDIA HICKSII

AZALEA ILEX GLABRA ILEX ROTUNDA

PIERIS JAPONICA

ENKIANTHUS CAMPANULATUS

AZALEA 'DAVIESI'

ILEX GREEN ISLAND

MALUS

HEDERA HELIX BALTICA

STYRAX JAPONICA

CORNUS MAS

KALMIA LATIFOLIA

EXISTING FAGUS

BERBERIS THUNBERGI

C O U R T

COMPOST AREA

RHODODENDRON 'BOULE DE NEIGE'

TAXUS CUSPIDATA NANA

TAXUS CUSPIDATA NANA

TSUGA CANADENSIS

BETULA PENDULA ALBA

BETULA PENDULA ALBA

TAXUS CUSPIDATA NANA

HEDERA HELIX

B R O O K

TSUGA CANADENSIS

I S L A N D

N

0 10 20 40'

7.
Windswept by the Sea

Seashore places have in common salt spray, drifting sand, and constant wind but plants to withstand these conditions can be found, and the seaside gardener soon learns how important it is to prepare the soil well for them. Watering and regular feeding are also necessary if the picturesque Japanese black pine, beach plum, and bayberry are to flourish.

Located on the dunes at the end of Long Island, this house designed by Eldridge Snyder, has a difficult location. Success has been due to the patience of the owners in developing a garden despite untoward conditions. Plans include a screen planting as protection from the road, a flower garden, and an open lawn for games. The beautiful round house, planned on two levels to fit the unusual site, is approached at the level of the road and most of the rooms are on a level with the dunes.

One garden, developed to the east, includes a lawn spacious enough for children to play without causing damage to the wide flower beds that surround it. Here plants indigenous to the seashore are massed to form a barrier against strong wind and to screen off the road. The more intimate flower garden is adjacent to the house with a spiral stairway leading directly to it from a balcony. From the foot of the stairs a wisteria climbs the cinder-block wall and grows luxuriantly on the protected west side.

Railroad ties form walls for the garden and the raised beds in which low junipers are planted with an occasional beach plum and Japanese black pine. Such walls are not difficult to construct and they hold the necessary depth of top soil, which is so important in any seaside planting where there may be nothing but sand. While certain plants do grow in sandy soil, and you may select these, still it is wise to provide plenty of rich top soil to insure a quick start for new plantings.

Beds are designed in a step-back pattern, following the line of the dunes. A wide bed for spring bulbs holds 'Red Emperor' and 'Glacier' tulips. These are followed by geraniums and begonias, both excellent at the seashore. Here geraniums sometimes bloom almost to Thanksgiving.

As native plants in the outside border grow thick and tall, they provide protection for the plants which are not native but have now been safely introduced. A number of hollies are being tested here with protection in winter. Snow-fencing has helped keep sand from drifting over the beds.

From dining room and service wing, large windows look out on the dunes. Directly below the windows there is a long narrow planting of junipers, bayberry, and beach plum that is much enjoyed from within.

When a garden is planned in such a location, the first thing is to establish beachgrass, *Ammophila arenaria,* in the surrounding area. Usually this can be easily accomplished by dividing existing clumps and setting them directly in the sand, but failing a supply, beachgrass can be bought. Once the clumps grow together, the sand does not shift and the new plantings beyond develop nicely.

68

At the bottom of the spiral stairway and beside the cinder-block wall, a young wisteria is being trained along the bottom of the railing. A raised bed holds a Japanese pine and low junipers, with annuals for cutting at the base of the wall. This bed was constructed to hide the area below the house and to keep sand from blowing through.

69

Broad steps made of railroad ties lead to the dunes where beach plum and bay-berry form a background for the garden. A wall of ties holds low junipers. Beds of pink and white geraniums and begonias are bright and colorful for months.

The step-back wall with junipers and beach plum makes an interesting pattern for this small garden. The 3-foot bed below the wall is filled in spring with early tulips and daffodils, later with geraniums edged with wax begonias.

Trees

Elaeagnus angustifolia	Russian olive
Pinus Thunbergii	Japanese black pine

Shrubs

Caryopteris incana	Bluebeard or blue spirea
Cotoneaster adpressa praecox	Creeping cotoneaster
horizontalis	Rockspray cotoneaster
Ilex, selected forms	Holly
Juniperus chinensis Sargentii	Sargent juniper
horizontalis plumosa	Plume or Andorra juniper
squamata Parsonii	Parson juniper
Ligustrum obtusifolium Regelianum	Regel privet
ovalifolium	California privet
Myrica pensylvanica	Bayberry
Prunus maritima	Beach plum
Rosa rugosa	Rugosa rose

Vines and groundcovers

Ammophila arenaria	Beachgrass
Wisteria sinensis	Chinese wisteria

Bulbs and bedding plants

Parson juniper makes a thick carpet in the built-up beds that are seen from the dining room. Bayberry and black pines are planted at the corners. Beyond the dunes is the invaluable beachgrass.

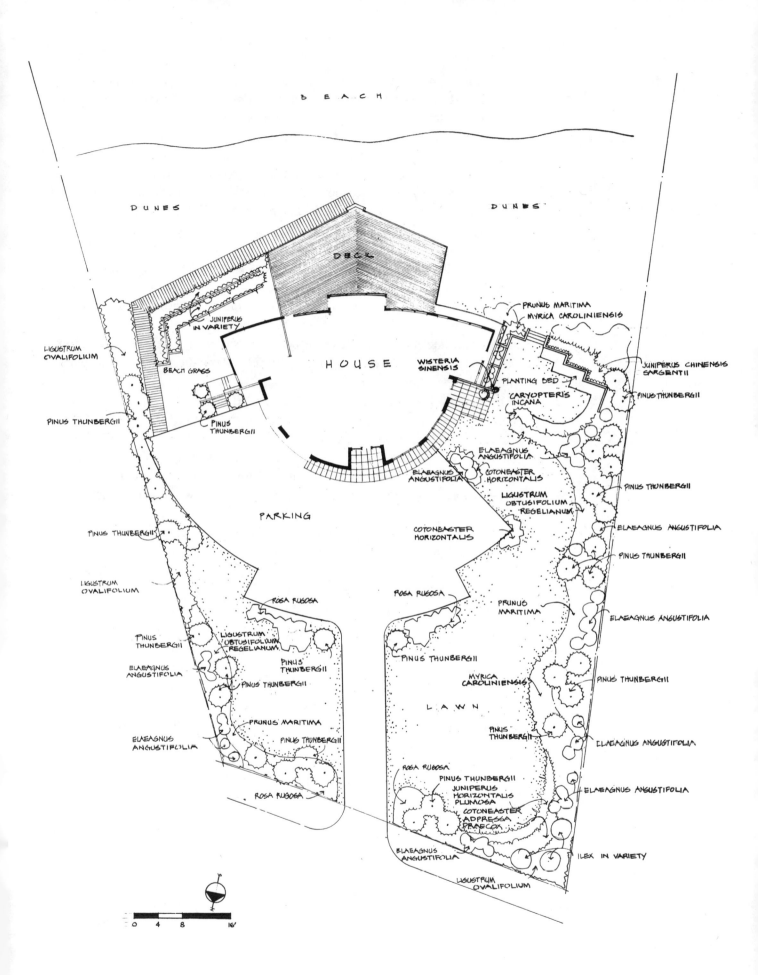

BEACH

DUNES   DUNES

DECK

PRUNUS MARITIMA
MYRICA CAROLINIENSIS

LIGUSTRUM
OVALIFOLIUM

JUNIPERUS
IN VARIETY

HOUSE

WISTERIA
SINENSIS

JUNIPERUS CHINENSIS
SARGENTII

BEACH GRASS

PLANTING BED

PINUS THUNBERGII

CARYOPTERIS
INCANA

PINUS THUNBERGII

PINUS
THUNBERGII

ELAEAGNUS
ANGUSTIFOLIA

ELAEAGNUS
ANGUSTIFOLIA

COTONEASTER
HORIZONTALIS

PINUS THUNBERGII

LIGUSTRUM
OBTUSIFOLIUM
REGELIANUM

ELAEAGNUS ANGUSTIFOLIA

PINUS THUNBERGII

COTONEASTER
HORIZONTALIS

PINUS THUNBERGII

PARKING

ROSA RUGOSA

ELAEAGNUS ANGUSTIFOLIA

LIGUSTRUM
OVALIFOLIUM

ROSA RUGOSA

PRUNUS
MARITIMA

PINUS
THUNBERGII

LIGUSTRUM
OBTUSIFOLIUM
REGELIANUM

PINUS THUNBERGII

ELAEAGNUS ANGUSTIFOLIA

PINUS
THUNBERGII

PINUS
THUNBERGII

MYRICA
CAROLINIENSIS

PINUS THUNBERGII

ELAEAGNUS
ANGUSTIFOLIA

PINUS THUNBERGII

LAWN

PINUS
THUNBERGII

ELAEAGNUS ANGUSTIFOLIA

PRUNUS MARITIMA

PINUS THUNBERGII

ROSA RUGOSA

ELAEAGNUS
ANGUSTIFOLIA

PINUS THUNBERGII

ELAEAGNUS ANGUSTIFOLIA

JUNIPERUS
HORIZONTALIS
PLUMOSA

COTONEASTER
ADPRESSA
PRAECOX

ROSA RUGOSA

ILEX IN VARIETY

ELAEAGNUS
ANGUSTIFOLIA

LIGUSTRUM
OVALIFOLIUM

0   4   8   16'

8.
Waterfront Cottage

For this property, 80 x 150 feet, situated on a point of land jutting into one of the Long Island bays but not directly on the dunes, a fairly wide selection of plants was possible. The small summer cottage faces southwest with a glorious view of the water and the advantage of prevailing southwest winds. The owners wanted a trim planting to enhance their simple cottage with a few roses, some perennials, annuals for color, and above all, plants that would flourish at the seashore. A basic design was evolved with a series of four garden rooms on the side protected from wind and hidden from passersby.

The approach to the house from the driveway is along a 4-foot-wide flagstone path that passes two of the gardens—roses on the left and annuals on the right. The sixteen rose plants backed by a yew hedge along the garage wall are in almost constant bloom through summer and fall. The annual garden, a 6 x 20-foot border opposite the front door, is also colorful through summer and late into fall with white petunias, sweet alyssum, blue ageratum, blue salvia, and masses of deep pink petunias. Here there are always plenty of flowers for cutting.

The narrow front porch is flanked by two dwarf boxwood and the taller Japanese holly. A fragrant viburnum grows near the guest-room door. Dwarf andromeda and pachysandra complete the low planting beneath the living-room window. At the corner of the house there is a grouping of Chinese dogwood with cherry-laurel and skimmia below. To the left of the entrance a breezeway, somewhat protected by a fence and yews, makes a delightful spot for dining when it is not too windy.

At the front, a wide bay with two Russian olives frames a 15-foot circular garden that is bordered with roundleaf holly, Douglas fir, and native red-cedars. This well protected evergreen garden is a comfortable place to sit when the wind blows in from the sea.

From the round garden a grass path with a dozen day-lilies and several clumps of iris leads to a perennial garden. A board fence protects this garden from sea breezes, and it encompasses about 400 square feet. A small central area of brick bordered by dwarf box makes a delightful place for sunning. The summer perennials give splashes of color to this quiet spot where a bird-bath that drips a few drops of water each second adds interest. This little sanctuary can be seen from the dining room through a planting of bitter-sweet and tamarisk, a good combination for the seashore.

Passing through the second garden gate, we come to the water's edge where the bank is covered with wild roses and beach plum. Several Japanese black pines along the property line give a feeling of enclosure. This pine will stand salt spray and wind better than any other and, as it grows, it develops an interesting form.

74

The approach became a garden with tall plants to give protection from wind. The path, wide enough for two to walk side-by-side, leads to a tiny porch, which is flanked by Japanese holly. A pair of dwarf English box—a gift from friends—with Japanese andromeda and pachysandra complete a composition beside the low steps. A Chinese dogwood shields the guest-room door.

75

From the breezeway, it is easy to pull out chairs to the lawn for sunning and enjoyment of the sea. Here a mass of marigolds with an espaliered pyracantha and Pfitzer juniper make a planting that withstands the strongest wind.

GOTTSCHO-SCHLEISNER PHOTO

A simple board fence encloses this blue-and-white garden, outlined with dwarf English box, and protects perennials and people from the wind.

This little garden with birdbath and dripping water is pleasant to gaze upon from the dining room.

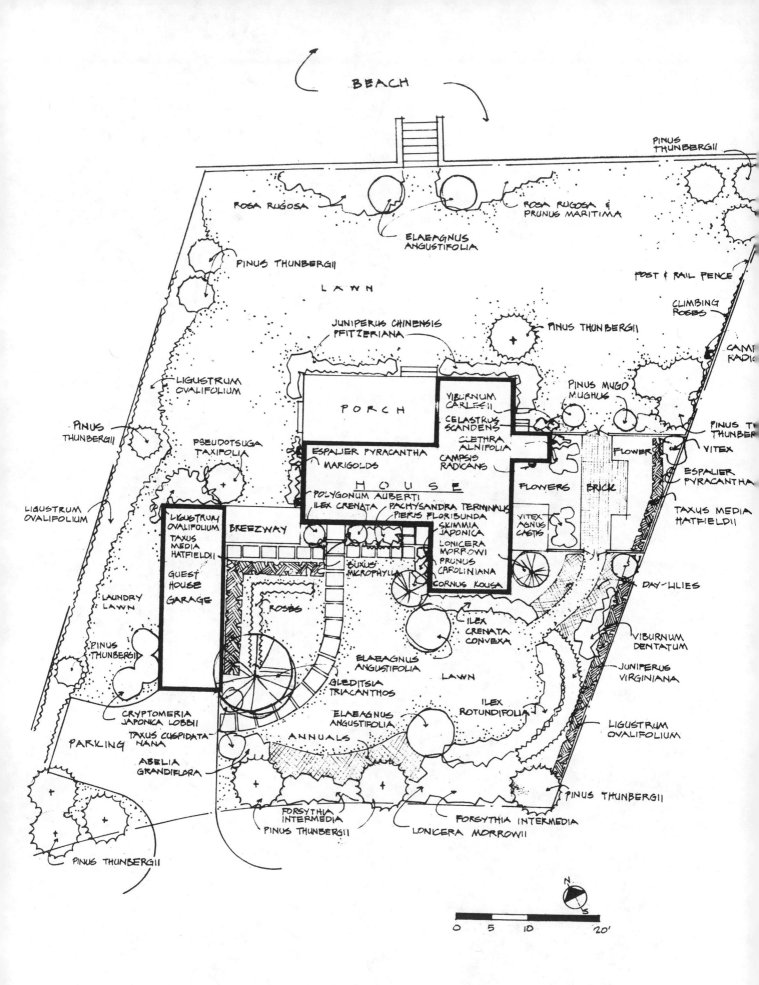

BEACH

PINUS THUNBERGII

ROSA RUGOSA

ROSA RUGOSA & PRUNUS MARITIMA

ELAEAGNUS ANGUSTIFOLIA

PINUS THUNBERGII

POST & RAIL FENCE

L A W N

CLIMBING ROSES

JUNIPERUS CHINENSIS PFITZERIANA

PINUS THUNBERGII

CAMP RADIC

LIGUSTRUM OVALIFOLIUM

PINUS MUGO MUGHUS

PORCH

VIBURNUM CARLESII

CELASTRUS SCANDENS

PINUS THUNBERGII

PSEUDOTSUGA TAXIFOLIA

CLETHRA ALNIFOLIA

FLOWER

PINUS THUNBER

VITEX

ESPALIER PYRACANTHA

ESPALIER PYRACANTHA MARIGOLDS

CAMPSIS RADICANS

FLOWERS

BRICK

H O U S E

LIGUSTRUM OVALIFOLIUM

POLYGONUM AUBERTI
ILEX CRENATA

PACHYSANDRA TERMINALS
PIERIS FLORIBUNDA

TAXUS MEDIA HATFIELDII

LIGUSTRUM OVALIFOLIUM
TAXUS MEDIA HATFIELDII

BREEZWAY

SKIMMIA JAPONICA

VITEX AGNUS CASTUS

GUEST HOUSE GARAGE

BUXUS MICROPHYLLA

LONICERA MORROWI
PRUNUS CAROLINIANA

CORNUS KOUSA

DAY-LILIES

ROSES

LAUNDRY LAWN

ILEX CRENATA CONVEXA

VIBURNUM DENTATUM

PINUS THUNBERGII

ELAEAGNUS ANGUSTIFOLIA

L A W N

JUNIPERUS VIRGINIANA

CRYPTOMERIA JAPONICA LOBBII

GLEDITSIA TRIACANTHOS

ILEX ROTUNDIFOLIA

LIGUSTRUM OVALIFOLIUM

TAXUS CUSPIDATA NANA

ELAEAGNUS ANGUSTIFOLIA

ABELIA GRANDIFLORA

A N N U A L S

PARKING

PINUS THUNBERGII

FORSYTHIA INTERMEDIA

PINUS THUNBERGII

FORSYTHIA INTERMEDIA

LONICERA MORROWII

PINUS THUNBERGII

N
S

0   5   10   20'

Trees

Cornus Kousa chinensis	Chinese dogwood
Cryptomeria japonica Lobbii	Japanese cryptomeria
Elaeagnus angustifolia	Russian olive
Gleditsia triacanthos	Honey-locust
Juniperus virginiana	Red-cedar
Pinus Thunbergii	Japanese black pine
Pseudotsuga taxifolia	Douglas-fir

Shrubs

Abelia grandiflora	Glossy abelia
Buxus microphylla	Dwarf box
Clethra alnifolia	Sweet pepperbush
Forsythia intermedia	Border forsythia
Ilex crenata	Japanese holly
convexa	Boxleaf holly
rotunda	Roundleaf holly
Juniperus chinensis Pfitzeriana	Pfitzer juniper
horizontalis 'Bar Harbor'	Bar Harbor juniper
Ligustrum ovalifolium	California privet
Lonicera Morrowii	Morrow honeysuckle
Pieris floribunda	Dwarf andromeda
Pinus Mugo Mughus	Mugho pine
Prunus caroliniana	Cherry-laurel
maritima	Beach plum
Rosa rugosa	Rugosa rose
Skimmia japonica	Japanese skimmia
Taxus media Hatfieldii	Hatfield yew
cuspidata nana	Dwarf Japanese yew
Viburnum Carlesii	Fragrant viburnum
dentatum	Arrow-wood
Vitex Agnus-castus	Chaste-tree

Vines and groundcovers

Campsis radicans	Trumpet-vine
Celastrus scandens	Bittersweet
Pachysandra terminalis	Japanese pachysandra
Polygonum Aubertii	Silver-lace or fleece-vine
Pyracantha coccinea Lalandii	Firethorn

Annuals, perennials, hybrid tea roses, day-lilies

9.

Small House Near the Ocean

Half a mile back from the ocean, this small house, designed by John Muller, was built in the middle of the large potato field on a plot 100 x 300 feet. Seashore conditions are not severe here so plant selection is fairly wide. There is still wind and salt spray but instead of drifting sand from the beaches, dust covers everything when the surrounding fields are plowed spring and fall. A planting screen around the property was therefore a necessity. The photographs taken fifteen years later show how well the planting has withstood hurricanes and wind.

The owner wanted plants reminiscent of her childhood in England, a property easy to maintain, and above all, privacy. Fast-growing trees for shade, terraces, flower border, toolhouse, and a vegetable garden were other requirements.

First a post-and-rail fence was erected on three sides and a double staggered row of Regel privet planted inside for screening. This particular privet, with jet-black berries that the pheasants enjoy, is excellent for many situations. Crabapples line the road—plants well suited to this location and in keeping with the low house. The front door, also the smaller kitchen door, are set off by Japanese andromeda, of good year-round appearance.

Shade was so important for this windy sunny acre that we went shopping for trees. First on the list was a beech, a truly English tree. This was the largest and most expensive item but it has proved well worth its cost for the joy of watching it grow. Birds flock to the dense protecting branches and grandchildren climb through the low branches. Our next selections were a pin oak to shade the terrace, a five-stemmed clump of gray birch for the front, and several Japanese black pines for winter interest at the corners.

As the terrace plan developed, we included garden areas for colorful bulbs and annuals inside along the house and outside following the line of the sitting wall. The typically English flower garden near the toolhouse is bright with flowers from early daffodils to late chrysanthemums. And the kitchen garden behind the wooden fence produces greens and small vegetables all through summer.

A multiple-stemmed gray birch planted to give shade at the front of this small house has developed beautifully. Japanese andromeda and Japanese hollies complete the planting here.

Akebia climbing up this porch trellis is an excellent vine with its five-starred leaves. In May the partially concealed plum-colored flowers open and are followed by small brown fruits. It needs pruning every year.

A post-and-rail fence with an occasional climbing rose breaks the line of vision to the road. Various flowering crabapples thicken the screen, and in bloom are a beautiful sight. Their autumn fruits add interest and bring the birds.

The flower garden includes a silk tree, Christmas-berry, viburnums, and sweet pepperbushes. In midsummer a mass of white phlox makes a fine showing and is especially attractive in the evening.

Trees

Albizzia Julibrissin	Silk-tree
Betula populifolia	Gray birch
Chionanthus virginica	Fringe-tree
Cornus florida	Flowering dogwood
Crataegus Phaenopyrum	Washington thorn
Elaeagnus angustifolia	Russian olive
Fagus sylvatica	European beech
Malus 'Dolgo'	Dolgo crabapple
floribunda	Showy crabapple
Arnoldiana	Arnold crabapple
Sargentii	Sargent crabapple
Photinia villosa	Christmas-berry
Pinus Thunbergii	Japanese black pine
Quercus palustris	Pin oak
Styrax japonica	Japanese snowbell-tree

Shrubs

Abelia grandiflora	Glossy abelia
Clethra alnifolia	Sweet pepperbush
Ilex crenata	Japanese holly
Ligustrum obtusifolium Regelianum	Regel privet
Pieris japonica	Japanese andromeda
Pyracantha coccinea Lalandii	Firethorn
Rhododendron 'Boule de Neige'	White rhododendron
Taxus cuspidata nana	Dwarf Japanese yew
Viburnum selected forms	

Vines

Akebia quinata	Five-leaf akebia
Campsis radicans 'Mme. Galen'	Trumpet-vine
Rosa 'New Dawn'	Climbing rose

Annuals, perennials, bulbs, bedding plants, vegetables

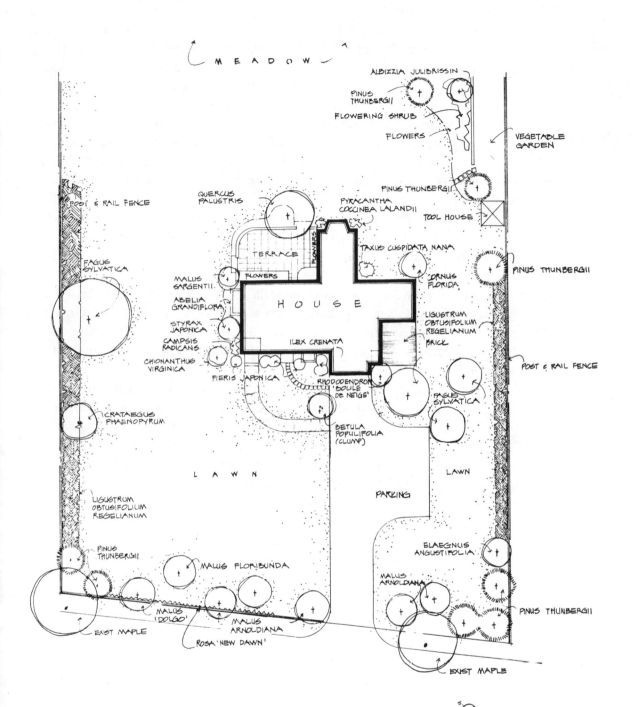

MEADOW

ALBIZZIA JULIBRISSIN

PINUS THUNBERGII

FLOWERING SHRUB

FLOWERS

VEGETABLE GARDEN

PINUS THUNBERGII

QUERCUS PALUSTRIS

POST & RAIL FENCE

PYRACANTHA COCCINEA LALANDII

TOOL HOUSE

TERRACE

TAXUS CUSPIDATA NANA

FAGUS SYLVATICA

PINUS THUNBERGII

FLOWERS

MALUS SARGENTII

CORNUS FLORIDA

ABELIA GRANDIFLORA

HOUSE

STYRAX JAPONICA

LIGUSTRUM OBTUSIFOLIUM REGELIANUM

CAMPSIS RADICANS

ILEX CRENATA

BRICK

CHIONANTHUS VIRGINICA

PIERIS JAPONICA

POST & RAIL FENCE

RHODODENDRON 'BOULE DE NEIGE'

FAGUS SYLVATICA

CRATAEGUS PHAENOPYRUM

BETULA POPULIFOLIA (CLUMP)

LAWN

LAWN

PARKING

LIGUSTRUM OBTUSIFOLIUM REGELIANUM

PINUS THUNBERGII

ELAEGNUS ANGUSTIFOLIA

MALUS FLORIBUNDA

MALUS ARNOLDIANA

PINUS THUNBERGII

MALUS 'DOLGO'

EXIST MAPLE

MALUS ARNOLDIANA

ROSA 'NEW DAWN'

EXIST MAPLE

0   5   10   20'

The flagstone terrace with a low brick sitting wall is shaded by a pin oak. Annuals inside and outside the wall make the terrace a pretty sight from the large picture window.

85

10.
Weekend
Cottage

Not far from the city in a tangle of woodland, a two-acre plot with many fine trees was carefully thinned and a small area cleared for building. The house, designed by Peter Paul Muller, was ideally situated on a gentle slope oriented for views and prevailing wind. Grading helped to adapt the house to the site with proper drainage for terraces and other level areas.

The requirements were informality, year-round effects from inside and out, and low upkeep. Lawn was kept to a minimum and gravel used extensively for terraces and paths. Three areas received particular attention: the entrance terrace and border, window garden and south terrace, and the woodland garden.

Since the front entrance is below the driveway, the approach is by way of 6-foot-wide steps that lead across a gravel terrace to the front door. This terrace with its raised beds is seen from the kitchen window and is lovely in all seasons.

Opposite, on the south, are two small flagstone terraces flanking the large picture windows, the only planting, two trumpet-vines on trellises. Gravel has been substituted for planting under the wide overhang and there are occasional ornamental containers for interest. A wide grassy area sloping to the woods is seen from the windows.

On the west the window garden with stylized raised beds is planted with cotoneasters and junipers, both of which stand summer heat. Winter heathers, species yellow *Crocus chrysanthus*, pale lavender *C. tomasinianus*, purple *C. vernus, N. triandrus,* and *Narcissus minimus* 'Silverbells' are planted for late winter and early spring. Hanging baskets of begonias 'Carl Hanz' bring summer color. From here a path leads into the woodland garden.

Each area has a character of its own with easy transitions from one to another provided by the plantings. There are flowers from very late winter until frost and then autumn brings the reds and purples of dogwoods, the yellow of the tulip trees, poplars, and birches, and later, the wine glow of oak and the pale yellow of autumn witchhazel.

Winter weekends offer other pictures—the hanging baskets turned into feeders attract many birds; forms of trees are revealed; and when the snow comes, the large dogwood and trumpet-creepers outside the picture windows are etched against the winter hillside. Clara Coffey, L.A.

A Japanese holly at the doorstep has fine structure and texture and requires only a summer pruning. At the left the creeping gray green juniper spreads over the gravel in which white violets and gray thyme are growing luxuriantly. A lavender wisteria climbs the louvered fence, and tubs of pink geraniums and white petunias bring summer color.

Railroad ties retain a 4-foot wide, 3-foot high bed with a background of hedge holly. Rockspray and bearberry, cotoneasters, creeping junipers, Baltic ivy, and sedums form a thick mat and make a tapestry of color in the bed and falling over the wall. All withstand drought, need little pruning, no weeding, and are a delight in every season. The lower bed, edged with weathered wood, is filled with lavender, spring bulbs, and forget-me-nots. Blue spirea and geraniums give summer bloom. The gray lavender, bronze junipers, and cotoneasters, and green ivy against the weathered ties make a lovely winter picture, too.

Trees

Acer saccharum	Sugar maple
Amelanchier canadensis	Shadbush
Pinus Strobus	White pine
Tsuga canadensis	Canada hemlock

Shrubs

Abelia grandiflora	Glossy abelia
Azalea indica alba	White
arborescens	Royal or sweet
mollis	Chinese
nudiflora	Pinxterbloom
Caryopteris incana	Bluebeard or blue spirea
Corylopsis spicata	Winter hazel
Cotoneaster horizontalis	Rockspray cotoneaster
Dammeri	Bearberry cotoneaster
Cydonia japonica	Flowering quince
Erica carnea, selected forms	Heath
Hamamelis mollis	Chinese witchhazel
virginiana	Autumn witchhazel
Ilex crenata	Japanese holly
verticillata	Winterberry (pistillate and staminate forms)
Juniperus, selected forms	Juniper
Kalmia angustifolia	Sheep-laurel
latifolia	Mountain-laurel
Lavandula officinalis	Lavender
Lindera aestivale	Benzoin or spicebush
Pyracantha coccinea Lalandii	Firethorn
Viburnum dentatum	Arrow-wood
Lentago	Nannyberry
prunifolium	Blackhaw

Vines and groundcovers

Campsis radicans	Trumpet-vine
Hedera Helix baltica	Baltic ivy
Vinca minor	Myrtle or periwinkle
Wisteria sinensis	Chinese wisteria

Bulbs, perennials, wild flowers

The 5-foot-wide wood-chip path edged with local stones leads to a wild garden shaded by oaks and dogwoods. Here in the spring beneath clouds of old white dogwood and shadbush are drifts of narcissus, species tulips, scillas, muscari, mertensia, primroses, and forget-me-nots. Along the path grow ginger (*Asarum*), epimedium, tiarella, Jacobs-ladder (*Polemonium reptans*), early *Phlox divaricata* and a number of ferns. In summer wood lilies (*Lilium philadelphicum*) and day-lilies (*Hemerocallis*) are colorful.

88

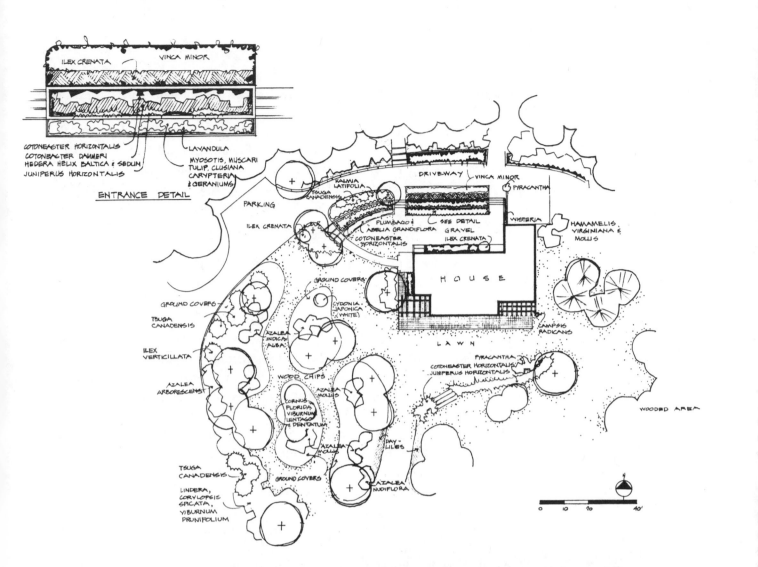

ILEX CRENATA   VINCA MINOR

COTONEASTER HORIZONTALIS
COTONEASTER DAMMERI
HEDERA HELIX BALTICA & SEDUM
JUNIPERUS HORIZONTALIS

LAVANDULA

MYOSOTIS, MUSCARI
TULIP, CLUSIANA
CARYPTERIA
& GERANIUMS

ENTRANCE DETAIL

PARKING

KALMIA
LATIFOLIA

TSUGA
CANADENSIS

ILEX CRENATA

PLUMBAGO &
ABELIA GRANDIFLORA

COTONEASTER
HORIZONTALIS

DRIVEWAY   VINCA MINOR

PYRACANTHA

SEE DETAIL
GRAVEL

ILEX CRENATA

WISTERIA

HAMAMELIS
VIRGINIANA &
MOLLIS

GROUND COVERS

GROUND COVERS

TSUGA
CANADENSIS

ILEX
VERTICILLATA

AZALEA
ARBORESCENS

TSUGA
CANADENSIS

LINDERA,
CORYLOPSIS
SPICATA,
VIBURNUM
PRUNIFOLIUM

CYDONIA
JAPONICA
(WHITE)

AZALEA
INDICA
ALBA

WOOD CHIPS

CORNUS
FLORIDA
VIBURNUM
LENTAGO
& DENTATUM

AZALEA
MOLLIS

AZALEA
MOLLIS

GROUND COVERS

DAY-
LILIES

AZALEA
NUDIFLORA

H O U S E

L A W N

CAMPSIS
RADICANS

PYRACANTHA
COTONEASTER HORIZONTALIS
JUNIPERUS HORIZONTALIS

WOODED AREA

0   10   20   40'

11.
Contemporary House

A modern house set halfway up a treeless hill was designed by the firm of Brown, Lawford, and Forbes for an older couple whose grandchildren were frequent visitors. The plot, 96 x 160 feet facing west, looked down on the road and houses below. The landscape plan included an attractive approach, trees for shade and screening, an open terrace at the back, small flower and vegetable gardens, a concealed laundry yard, open space where the children could run and slide, and above all, low maintenance. Grading at front and rear provided level areas for terraces. Walls of beautiful stone were built to incorporate the terraces in the design.

Seven trees were planted between house and street for shade and screening. In front of the large living-room windows a honey-locust was placed where its handsome structure could be fully seen, and here it interrupts the line of vision toward the busy road. For the hill, two European beech trees were chosen; these are always beautiful with their gray bark and russet leaves held far into the winter. Near the street, two sweet gum trees were placed to accent the driveway entrance; by the garage and service wing, clumps of white birch with hemlocks to hide the garage next door. All except the beeches have grown quite rapidly.

The front door in the corner of the house is hidden from the driveway but a wide step-ramp is invitation to the upper level. Dwarf yews outline the base of the house and three have grown together by the entrance to the ramp. On the upper level, a three-stemmed birch clump stands near the wall. Over the years this upper terrace, designed as a green garden with white birches, dwarf hollies, and white-flowering evergreen azaleas, has become increasingly attractive and it is easy to maintain.

Abelias are in almost constant bloom beside the house and a sorrel-tree makes a good accent. American hollies along the property line are for winter effect and protection. From the corner there is a charming view of the gentle slope at the rear of the property, a perfect setting for pink and white azaleas and white rhododendrons. The bedrooms look out on this slope where the arching branches of Zabel cotoneaster will not grow above the window sills. Under the wide overhang there is a 3-foot gravel strip.

The flagstone terrace looks across a small lawn and beyond a sugar maple —selected for shape and color—to the stone retaining wall. In one corner a blue Atlas cedar gives winter color and in the other a star magnolia offers lovely spring blossoms. Behind the wall is the vegetable garden.

A walk up the step-ramp offers views of the attractive low house settled so beautifully into the hillside and surrounded by plantings that can be enjoyed in every season.

90

The planting as it was just completed. NEUHOF PHOTO

Ten years later, the honey-locust has grown beautifully and clumps of white birch on the terrace frame the doorway. Dwarf yews planted along the steps have grown together into a hedge that needs no shearing. Boxleaf hollies and azaleas inside the wall are an evergreen mass in winter, a picture of white flowers in spring.

Dwarf yews below the window make an enduring green line that will not grow above the sill. NEUHOF PHOTO

The terrace, newly planted, opens out from the living room and is planted with dwarf hollies and fragrant doublefile viburnums, this with white flowers in spring and red-to-black September fruits. There is a 3-foot spread of gravel adjacent to the building—an area where it is impossible to grow plants. Beyond the wide gutter, Zabel cotoneasters extend the full length of the house. NEUHOF PHOTO

The dwarf yews at the entrance steps are now full grown, and the low boxleaf holly surrounds the birch.

Trees

Acer rubrum	Red maple
saccharum	Sugar maple
Betula pendula alba	White birch
Castanea mollissima	Chinese chestnut
Cedrus atlantica glauca	Blue Atlas cedar
Crataegus Crus-galli	Cockspur thorn
Fagus sylvatica	European beech
Gleditsia triacanthos	Honey-locust
Ilex opaca	American holly
Liquidambar Styraciflua	Sweet gum
Magnolia stellata	Star magnolia
Malus Sargentii	Sargent crabapple
Oxydendrum arboreum	Sourwood or sorrel-tree
Quercus palustris	Pin oak
Tsuga canadensis	Canada hemlock

Shrubs

Abelia grandiflora	Glossy abelia
Azalea arborescens	Royal or sweet azalea
indica alba	White evergreen azalea
Cotoneaster divaricata	Spreading cotoneaster
horizontalis	Rockspray cotoneaster
Zabelii	Zabel cotoneaster
Forsythia suspensa	Drooping forsythia
Ilex crenata	Japanese holly
convexa	Boxleaf holly
Helleri	Heller holly
glabra	Inkberry
opaca	American holly
Leucothoe Catesbaei	Drooping leucothoe
Ligustrum obtusifolium Regelianum	Regel privet
Rhododendron 'Boule de Neige'	Dwarf white
Syringa vulgaris	Common lilac
Taxus cuspidata nana	Dwarf Japanese yew
capitata	Upright yew
Vaccinium corymbosum	Highbush blueberry
Viburnum Carlesii	Fragrant viburnum
dilatatum	Linden viburnum
Lantana	Wayfaring-tree
Lentago	Nannyberry
tomentosum sterile	Japanese snowball

Groundcover

Vinca minor	Myrtle or periwinkle

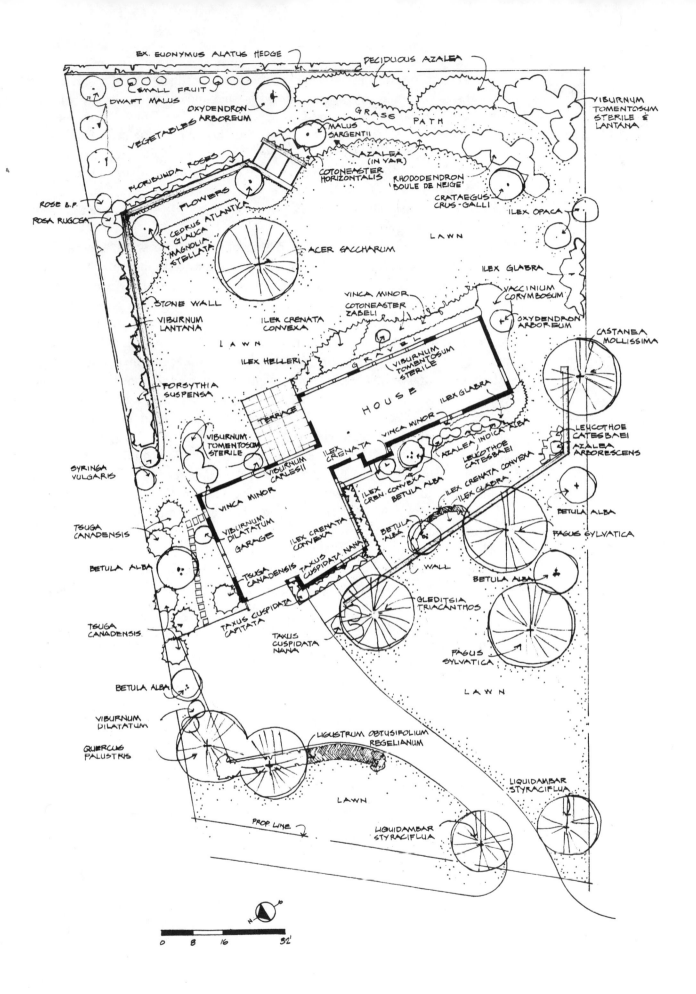

12.
Colonial
House

A two-acre site on the Connecticut shore with a fine view of Long Island Sound was originally an open field with one ancient elm, an old linden, some large Japanese yews, and a Scotch pine. The house, designed by Julian Fay, was placed close to the eastern boundary because of an easement requiring that a view of the water be kept open for the neighbor at the back. The landscape plan had to start from scratch and included: driveway and entrance court, trees to frame the house, a large terrace to overlook the Sound for entertaining, a small terrace off the bedroom for privacy, also rose and wild-flower gardens.

On one side, plants were selected that could endure wind and salt air; in general, attractiveness in summer was emphasized, the time when the house is most in use. Roses, the favorite flower of the owners, were planted wherever possible.

The gravel driveway leads up to the front of the house, where a wide brick platform extends the width of the garden. Two Chinese dogwoods, flanking this landing area, give white bloom in June and in maturity interesting structural forms. (The photographs show the planting in its second year.)

Behind the brick platform, a low hedge of boxleaf holly encloses a small entrance garden filled with white azaleas and blue myrtle, a Japanese maple accenting one corner. In pockets through the myrtle, white tulips 'Diana' give a mass of bloom in May from new bulbs planted each October. Against the great chimney, a climbing hydrangea, perfect for this northern exposure, will in time climb to the very top and produce effective panicles of white flowers through summer.

Upright yews enclose the service wing and numerous wild flowers that do not require sun thrive in this shaded area which is in view of the kitchen window. There is always something there in bud or flower. The toolhouse, a part of the garage, has a door opening onto the driveway; to hide this, Japanese hollies were planted at the end of the building. Around the service court we would have preferred trees, but because of the easement, Pfitzer junipers were planted around the edge. A hawthorn with red berries that hold into winter grows at the corner and a flowering crabapple near the terrace.

The three terraces are used in quite different ways. The brick dining terrace was constructed off the kitchen, is convenient for serving, has a view of the Sound, and is sheltered by a hedge of dwarf Japanese yew.

A flagstone walk bordered with roses leads from the small dining terrace to a larger entertaining terrace in the center. This much-frequented path is a source of pleasure all through summer when the roses are blooming. It is attractive from inside the house, too, and there are enough plants to have roses to pick for the house and to give away.

The larger flagstone terrace is sheltered between the wings of the house and shaded by two honey-locusts. Their lacy branching habit makes them

96

perfect here and they are pruned high so as not to obstruct the view of the water. Below the terrace wall, the arching branches of glossy abelia open pink-and-white flowers from mid-July to November. The evergreen euonymus planted against the stucco wall will soon form a green background. On the lawn outside the terrace, three pin oaks offer shade and make lovely shadows on the lawn.

The third terrace off the master bedroom is small, and it too provides a fine view of the water. Three feet above the grade with its own little garden of fragrant plants, this looks through branches of an apple tree to the rose garden below.

The approach to the house goes past the service court, which is enclosed by low junipers and terminates in a wide brick platform. The entrance is set off by Chinese dogwoods.

The low hedge of boxleaf holly conceals a delightful entrance garden planted with myrtle and hundreds of white tulips. In the corner there is a Japanese maple and white azaleas grow below the bedroom window. In time a climbing hydrangea will cover the large chimney.

On this facade that faces the water two honey-locusts frame a lovely view, and a rose walk connects the dining terrace with a terrace sheltered by the wings of the house.

The small bedroom terrace, raised 3 feet above the existing grade, looks through the apple tree to roses that have since been planted below. The wide bed on the terrace now includes 'The Fairy' rose and fragrant annuals—nicotiana and sweet alyssum— with an edging of strawberries.

Trees

Acer palmatum	Japanese maple
Cornus florida	Flowering dogwood
Kousa chinensis	Chinese dogwood
Crataegus Crus-galli	Cockspur thorn or hawthorn
Gleditsia triancanthos	Honey-locust
Malus floribunda	Showy crabapple
Pinus Strobus	White pine
Quercus palustris	Pin oak
Tsuga canadensis	Canada hemlock

Shrubs

Abelia grandiflora	Glossy abelia
Azalea 'Delaware Valley White'	
Caryopteris incana	Bluebeard or blue spirea
Ilex crenata convexa	Boxleaf holly
Juniperus chinensis Pfitzeriana	Pfitzer juniper
Pyracantha coccinea Lalandii	Firethorn
Taxus cuspidata	Japanese yew
nana	Dwarf Japanese yew
media Hatfieldii	Hedge yew
Vaccinium corymbosum	Highbush blueberry
Viburnum Carlesii	Fragrant viburnum
Sieboldii	Siebold viburnum

Vines and groundcover

Euonymus Fortunei	Climbing euonymus
Hydrangea petiolaris	Climbing hydrangea
Vinca minor	Myrtle or periwinkle

Roses, bulbs, annuals, wild flowers, strawberries

Outside the kitchen a small brick terrace level with the porch is often used for serving meals to grandchildren. The upright yews will grow into a hedge and the flowering crabapple will eventually tower over the hedge and be a splash of color as well as a screen for the distant road. It is from here that a flagstone path lined with roses and bordered with sweet alyssum leads to the main terrace.

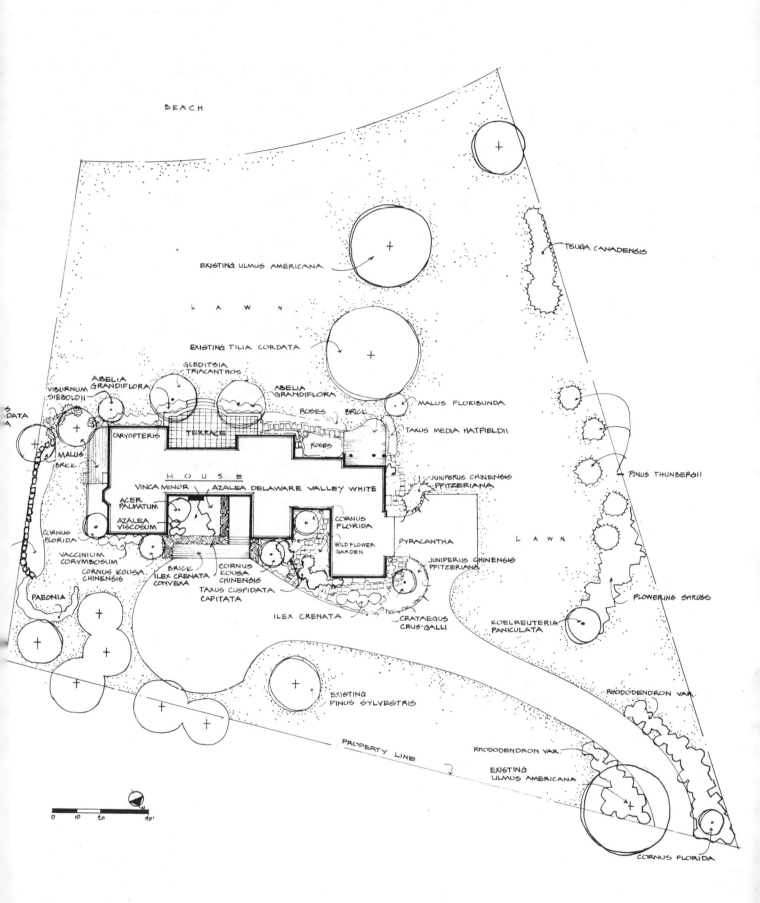

BEACH

TSUGA CANADENSIS

EXISTING ULMUS AMERICANA

L A W N

EXISTING TILIA CORDATA

ABELIA
GRANDIFLORA

GLEDITSIA
TRIACANTHOS

ABELIA
GRANDIFLORA

VIBURNUM
SIEBOLDII

ROSES   BRICK   MALUS FLORIBUNDA

S DATA

CARYOPTERIS   TERRACE   ROSES   TAXUS MEDIA HATFIELDII

MALUS
BRICK

H O U S E

JUNIPERUS CHINENSIS
PFITZERIANA

VINCA MINOR   AZALEA DELAWARE VALLEY WHITE

ACER
PALMATUM

CORNUS
FLORIDA   CORNUS
FLORIDA   L A W N

AZALEA
VISCOSUM   WILD FLOWER
GARDEN   PYRACANTHA

VACCINIUM
CORYMBOSUM   PINUS THUNBERGII

CORNUS KOUSA
CHINENSIS   BRICK
ILEX CRENATA
CONVEXA   CORNUS
KOUSA
CHINENSIS   JUNIPERUS CHINENSIS
PFITZERIANA

TAXUS CUSPIDATA
CAPITATA   FLOWERING SHRUBS

PAEONIA

ILEX CRENATA   CRATAEGUS
CRUS-GALLI   KOELREUTERIA
PANICULATA

EXISTING
PINUS SYLVESTRIS

RHODODENDRON VAR

PROPERTY LINE   RHODODENDRON VAR

EXISTING
ULMUS AMERICANA

0 10 20   40'   CORNUS FLORIDA

13.
Small Place for Enthusiastic Gardeners

On a plot 85 x 125 feet in a well-established neighborhood, a modified traditional house met local requirements by lining up with other dwellings on the block. This gave an ample front area for trees and planting about the house. The space in the back is not large but the garden-minded owners have utilized it to include most of the plants and features they wanted. They themselves made the plantings from an original professional plan that was somewhat altered in the working out. They wanted a design that would offer interest through the year with space for outdoor living—a terrace at ground level and a garden for flowers.

In front a pair of pin oaks provided quick shade and a frame for the house. A flowering dogwood screens a bedroom window on the left. Japanese holly and red azaleas soften the foundation line and, now that they are established, require only yearly pruning and feeding.

On the garden side a rectangular terrace with access from the kitchen is laid in sand and bordered with stone to emphasize the outline. Beyond there is an ample lawn and wide beds for hollies, rhododendrons, and azaleas.

Near the terrace a small pool was built with a spouting fountain, a refreshing sight and sound in summer. Gray artemesia and sedum add to this picture. Two trees were planted to give privacy. A columnar beech with full foliage cuts off the view of the neighbors and grows slowly enough not to get out of hand on a small property. A Chinese dogwood interrupts the long line of the garage roof and also conceals the graveled drying yard.

Across the lawn and opposite the terrace shrub and flower beds are outlined with small plants of dwarf English box which will eventually grow into a continuous green edge, a unifying factor for this small garden. There is long bloom from the early pinkshell azalea to the late 'J. T. Lovett', and they are all attractive in winter. A small patterned garden on the right holds many favorites for cutting and a few tomatoes, too.

Pin oaks make a welcoming approach, shade the house, and frame the entrance. A flowering dogwood gives privacy for a bedroom window and holly and azaleas complete a simple planting. When these plants grow together the effect will be uniform.

The dense, slow-growing, blue-green Waterer pine makes an excellent focal point for this small formal garden. Two low mugho pines accent the entrance, and the path is of the same flagstone as the terrace. Behind the low wall are two more mugho pines; colorful geraniums are used for bedding.

To get more room for plants a narrow bay was extended out from the end of the house. Dwarf boxwood provides the unifying element; background plantings are of Japanese maple; deep pink azaleas give color in spring. Miniature pink dahlias, 'Hazel Harper' and 'Jerry Hoek' fill in spaces among the new azaleas.

Trees

Acer palmatum	Japanese maple
Betula papyrifera	Paper birch
Cornus florida	Flowering dogwood
Kousa chinensis	Chinese dogwood
mas	Cornelian-cherry
Fagus sylvatica fastigiata	Columnar beech
Pinus Banksiana	Jack pine
Watereri	Waterer pine
Mugo Mughus	Mugho pine
Quercus palustris	Pin oak

Shrubs

Azalea 'Bridesmaid'	Pink
'Coral Bells'	Coral
'J. T. Lovett'	Deep pink
macrantha	Red
Vaseyi	Pinkshell azalea
Buxus microphylla	Dwarf box
koreana	Korean box
Elaeagnus pungens	Thorny-Russian-olive
Ilex Aquifolium	English holly
cornuta Burfordii	Burford holly
crenata	Japanese holly
Helleri	Heller holly
microphylla	Littleleaf holly
opaca	American holly
Wilsonii	Wilson holly
Kalmia latifolia	Mountain-laurel
Ligustrum lucidum	Glossy privet
Osmanthus ilicifolius	Holly olive
Photinia serrulata	Chinese photinia
Pinus Mugo Mughus	Mugho pine
Rhododendron 'Boule de Neige'	Dwarf white
'Windbeam'	Pink
Skimmia japonica	Japanese skimmia

Groundcover

Vinca minor	Myrtle or periwinkle

Perennials, dahlias, bedding plants, tomatoes

104

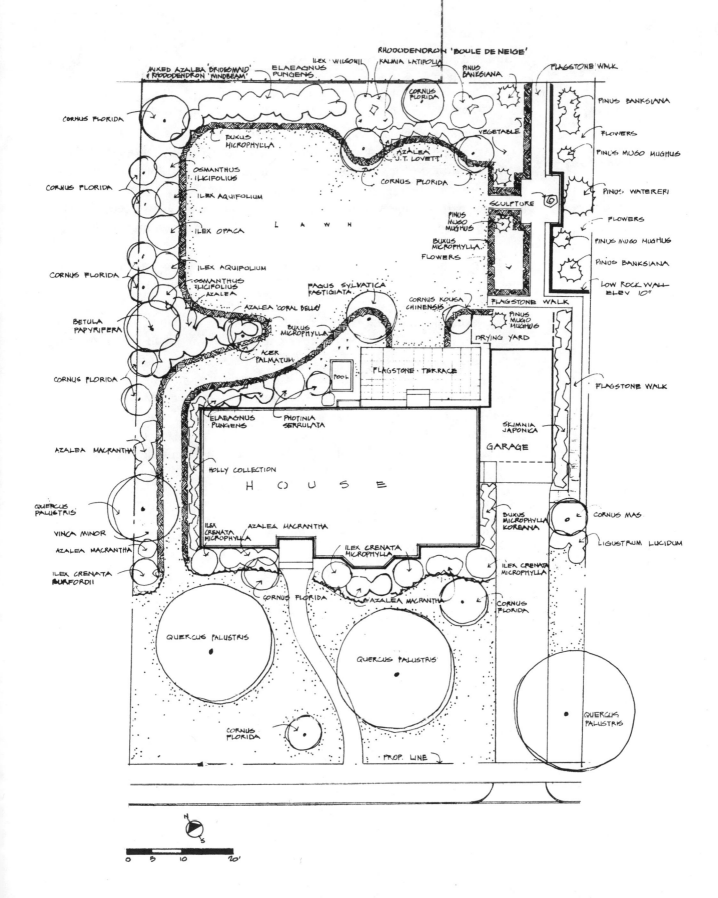

MIXED AZALEA 'BRIDESMAID' & RHODODENDRON 'WINDBEAM'

ELAEAGNUS PUNGENS

ILEX WILSONII

RHODODENDRON 'BOULE DE NEIGE'

KALMIA LATIFOLIA

PINUS BANKSIANA

FLAGSTONE WALK

CORNUS FLORIDA

BUXUS MICROPHYLLA

OSMANTHUS ILICIFOLIUS

ILEX AQUIFOLIUM

ILEX OPACA

ILEX AQUIFOLIUM

OSMANTHUS ILICIFOLIUS AZALEA

AZALEA 'CORAL BELLS'

BUXUS MICROPHYLLA

ACER PALMATUM

BETULA PAPYRIFERA

CORNUS FLORIDA

AZALEA MACRANTHA

QUERCUS PALUSTRIS

VINCA MINOR

AZALEA MACRANTHA

ILEX CRENATA BURFORDII

CORNUS FLORIDA

CORNUS FLORIDA

CORNUS FLORIDA

CORNUS FLORIDA

CORNUS FLORIDA

AZALEA 'J.T. LOVETT'

CORNUS FLORIDA

L A W N

VEGETABLE

SCULPTURE

PINUS MUGO MUGHUS

BUXUS MICROPHYLLA

FLOWERS

FLAGSTONE WALK

PINUS BANKSIANA

FLOWERS

PINUS MUGO MUGHUS

PINUS WATERERI

FLOWERS

PINUS MUGO MUGHUS

PINUS BANKSIANA

LOW ROCK WALL ELEV 10"

FAGUS SYLVATICA FASTIGIATA

CORNUS KOUSA CHINENSIS

PINUS MUGO MUGHUS

DRYING YARD

POOL

FLAGSTONE · TERRACE

ELAEAGNUS PUNGENS

PHOTINIA SERRULATA

FLAGSTONE WALK

SKIMMIA JAPONICA

GARAGE

HOLLY COLLECTION

H O U S E

ILEX CRENATA MICROPHYLLA

AZALEA MACRANTHA

ILEX CRENATA MICROPHYLLA

AZALEA MACRANTHA

BUXUS MICROPHYLLA KOREANA

CORNUS MAS

LIGUSTRUM LUCIDUM

ILEX CRENATA MICROPHYLLA

CORNUS FLORIDA

QUERCUS PALUSTRIS

QUERCUS PALUSTRIS

QUERCUS PALUSTRIS

CORNUS FLORIDA

PROP. LINE

0   5   10   20'

14. Remodeled Salt Box

Situated in the Berkshire hills, this attractive salt box, remodeled by Dean Brown, perfectly suits a city couple who yearned for a secluded, quiet place in the country. "A Blade of Grass" is the name of this lovely home nestled among pines and old birches. Again, low maintenance was essential. Then the list included a proper approach and parking area for family and visitors, screen planting for first-floor bedroom windows, swimming pool and dressing rooms, terrace for outdoor dining with easy access to kitchen and living room, suitable planting for a rock ledge, small herb and vegetable garden, a "secret garden," annuals for cutting, and finally lots of bird feeders. This was a big order for a small property but with careful planning everything was included.

The new flagstone walk to the front door leads from an entrance gate and parking area along a lilac-lined border filled in spring with daffodils. Later, day-lilies give months of summer bloom.

The swimming pool located five steps below the terrace is small but convenient and a joy all summer. Part of the garage was made into a dressing room. The flagstone terrace with a low sitting wall follows the lines of the pool. The terrace with entrances from both living room and kitchen is spacious enough for entertaining. An old double white pine gives shade on the south and a fast-growing transplanted red maple will soon make the terrace cool enough for midday dining.

In the front a rock ledge is planted with rockspray cotoneasters, sedums, blue phlox, and ferns, a pretty sight from the living room. Just below the outcrop is the secret garden, a jungle when we started, but now designed with three beds of summer perennials. A wide step-ramp leads down to this. Viburnums, hawthorns, and evergreens, as well as bird-feeders, offer abundance to chickadees, junkos, goldfinches, cedar waxwings, mourning doves, and cardinals.

Flowering crabapples, with an underplanting of myrtle, shade bedrooms from afternoon sun. One large viburnum, the high-bush cranberry, fills the corner and makes a fine bird-feeding station. STRAUSS PHOTO

By the dining-room bay window on the left, one old lilac still towers to the second floor. On the right, a native hawthorn offers a nesting place for birds. Dwarf Japanese yews accent the entrance porch with clumps of mountain-laurel and a ground-cover of myrtle tying the planting together. STRAUSS PHOTO

Outside the living room and kitchen is a flagstone terrace with a low sitting wall beside the pool. Against the fence a young white pine and flowering dogwood are growing with Glendale azaleas and a bedding of bugleweed. A wisteria is being trained over the arch of the porch beside the dressing room. Hemlocks soften the corner by the gate.

STRAUSS PHOTO

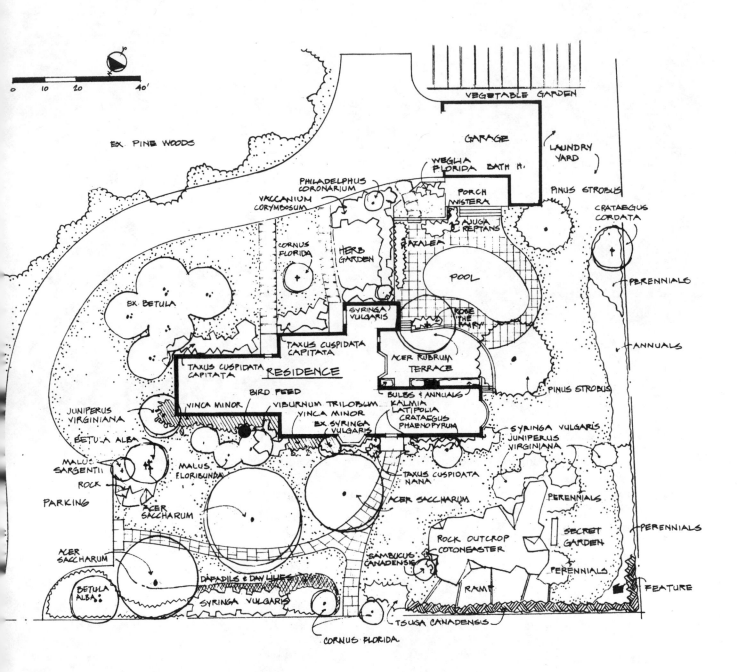

The step-ramp of railroad ties with a 4-inch mulch of pine needles and the post-and-rail fence, both well suited to this woodland setting, lead to the secret garden. One one side woodland plants, violets and ferns, grow near the rock and below the old cedar; on the other, clumps of hemlock shield the road. STRAUSS PHOTO

108

Trees

Acer rubrum	Red maple
saccharum	Sugar maple
Betula pendula alba	White birch
Cornus florida	Flowering dogwood
Crataegus Phaenopyrum	Washington thorn
Malus floribunda	Showy crabapple
Sargentii	Sargent crabapple
Pinus Strobus	White pine
Tsuga canadensis	Canada hemlock

Shrubs

Azalea Glendale Hybrids	
Cotoneaster horizontalis	Rockspray cotoneaster
Kalmia latifolia	Mountain-laurel
Philadelphus coronarius	Mock-orange
Sambucus canadensis	Elderberry
Syringa vulgaris	Common lilac
Taxus cuspidata capitata	Upright yew
nana	Dwarf Japanese yew
media	Hybrid yew
Vaccinium corymbosum	Highbush blueberry
Viburnum trilobum	Highbush cranberry
Weigela florida	Pink weigela

Vine and groundcover

Ajuga reptans	Bugleweed
Vinca minor	Myrtle or periwinkle
Wisteria sinensis	Chinese wisteria

15. Plant Collectors' Property

On a half-acre plot in a subdivision a couple who enjoy plants have collected an unusual number of azaleas, hollies, and rhododendrons. In spite of so many plants, over the years they have developed a design that makes this 100 x 150-foot lot appear a spacious setting for their home. Since the house is situated on a busy corner, they used their plants as a barrier against the constant flow of traffic and the noise of children in a school next door. The wide beds include evergreens as well as pink, white, lavender, and yellow azaleas and rhododendrons. Many of these, and also groundcovers, are propagated in a small greenhouse.

A stepping-stone path leads from the sidewalk to a raised brick terrace at the front door; a flowering dogwood in the breezeway corner casts shadow patterns on it. Along the sidewalk a hedge of English holly provides an evergreen enclosure. Between house and hedge an apple tree is colorful with spring blossoms and gives shade to living-room and bedroom windows through summer. An espaliered American holly, in nice association and with bright red berries that hold all winter, covers the space beside bedroom windows near the street.

A sugar maple selected for its high branching habit and bright fall hues softens the end of the house and makes a pleasant shadow on the lawn. Across the lawn and through plantings of rhododendrons and hollies are the greenhouse and work area at the rear of the property. Large specimens of American holly and white pine conceal the greenhouse and vary the skyline of the wide planting.

A white pine, pruned high to give shade, stands beside the flagstone dining terrace, which is 2 feet above the grass area. Beneath this tree in a groundcover of English ivy is a large rock hollowed out to hold water for the birds. Against the house low beds of Korean box and dwarf holly make an evergreen planting in scale and thriving despite the shade.

From this terrace three wide steps lead to a lower area for sunning and garden viewing. The sitting wall provided by the raised beds is used all year and behind it tall hollies and an arresting lacebark pine block out the school.

To provide circulation for the property, there is a narrow path that goes around the garage. A hemlock hedge and dwarf rhododendrons at the property line insure privacy on that side. Even the driveway is well hidden by a large American holly underplanted with azaleas and rhododendrons. Here the nurseryman, Henry Feil has planted a collection that also serves to make a delightful landscape design.

This evergreen planting of dwarf holly, spreading English yew, and, by the window, Japanese holly has the great advantage of not growing out of scale through the years and of remaining green throughout the year.

110

This front planting consists of a McIntosh apple tree moved in a large size to give immediate shade and privacy for the picture window. The holly hedge makes an excellent sidewalk barrier and needs only one light yearly trimming. A dwarf white pine, almost maximum size when planted, dominates the corner with pachistima as groundcover. This low evergreen has fine-toothed leaves that stay dark green through winter in good contrast to the blue-green of the pine.

Trees

Acer saccharum	Sugar maple
Cedrus atlantica glauca	Blue Atlas cedar
Chamaecyparis obtusa nana	Hinoki false-cypress
Cornus florida	Flowering dogwood
Ilex altaclarensis camelliaefolia	Camellia-leaf holly
Aquifolium	English holly
opaca	American holly
Koelreuteria paniculata	Goldenrain-tree
Malus 'McIntosh'	Apple-tree
'Red Jade'	Weeping crabapple
spectabilis 'Rosea plena'	Chinese crabapple
Pinus Bungeana	Lacebark pine
Strobus	White pine
nana	Dwarf white pine
Styrax Obassia	Fragrant snowbell-tree
Tsuga canadensis	Canada hemlock

Shrubs

Azalea 'Balsaminaeflorum'	Pale red
'Fairy Bells'	Pink
'Gumpo'	Dwarf white
indica alba	White
'Louise Gable'	Peach
Buxus sempervirens suffruticosa	Dwarf English box
microphylla koreana	Korean box
Daphne Genkwa	Lilac daphne
Hedera Helix conglomerata	English ivy
'Curlylocks'	
deltoidea	
'Maple Queen'	
'238th Street'	
Ilex Aquiperni 'Brilliant'	Chinese holly
crenata	Japanese holly
microphylla	Littleleaf holly
rugosa	Dwarf holly
Rhododendron	
'A. Bedford'	Pink
'Black Beauty'	Dark purple
'Blue Peter'	Purple
'Blue Tit'	Lavender
'Bow Bells'	Dwarf pink
'Goldsworth Yellow'	Pale yellow
'Keiskei'	Dwarf yellow
'Ramapo'	Dwarf violet
'Roslyn'	Lavender
'Sapphire'	Lavender
'Vulcan'	Bright red
'Wheatley'	Pink
Taxus baccata repandens	Spreading English yew

Vines and groundcovers

Hedera Helix	English ivy
baltica	Baltic ivy
Pachistima Canbyi	
Vinca minor	Myrtle or periwinkle

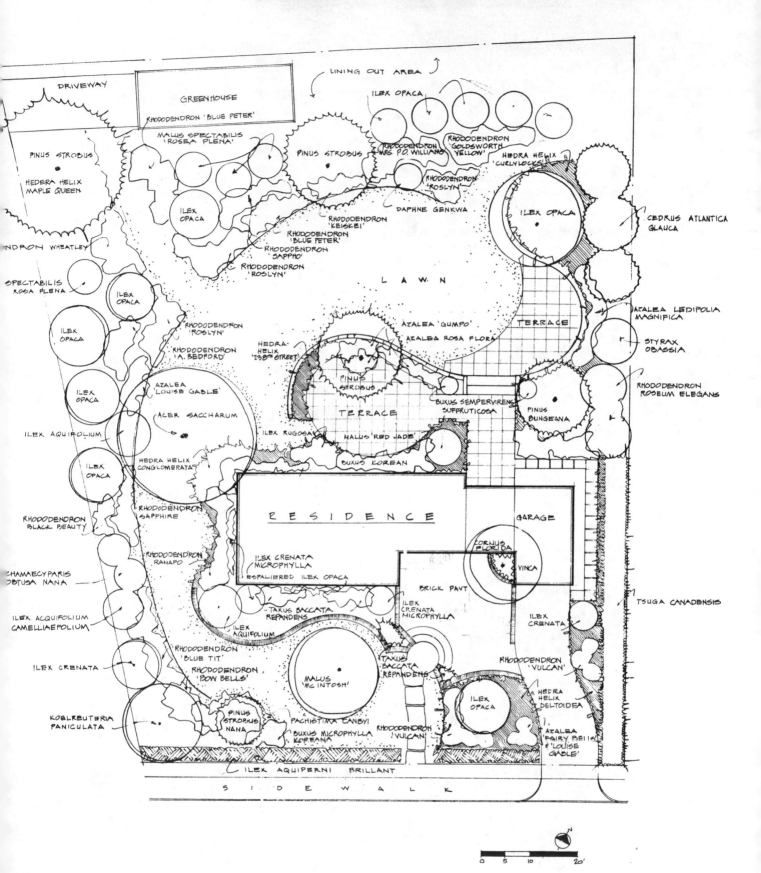

DRIVEWAY

GREENHOUSE

RHODODENDRON 'BLUE PETER'

MALUS SPECTABILIS 'ROSEA PLENA'

PINUS STROBUS

LINING OUT AREA

ILEX OPACA

PINUS STROBUS

RHODODENDRON 'MRS. P.O. WILLIAMS'

RHODODENDRON 'GOLDSWORTH YELLOW'

HEDRA HELIX 'CURLYLOCKS'

RHODODENDRON 'ROSLYN'

ILEX OPACA

CEDRUS ATLANTICA GLAUCA

PINUS STROBUS

HEDERA HELIX MAPLE QUEEN

ILEX OPACA

DAPHNE GENKWA

RHODODENDRON 'KEISKEI'

RHODODENDRON 'BLUE PETER'

RHODODENDRON 'SAPPHO'

RHODODENDRON 'ROSLYN'

L A W N

AZALEA 'GUMPO'

AZALEA ROSA FLORA

TERRACE

AZALEA LEDIPOLIA MAGNIFICA

NDRON WHEATLEY

SPECTABILIS ROSA PLENA

ILEX OPACA

RHODODENDRON 'ROSLYN'

ILEX OPACA

RHODODENDRON 'A. BEDFORD'

HEDRA HELIX '238TH STREET'

PINUS STROBUS

STYRAX OBASSIA

ILEX OPACA

AZALEA 'LOUISE GABLE'

TERRACE

BUXUS SEMPERVIRENS SUFFRUTICOSA

RHODODENDRON ROSEUM ELEGANS

ACER SACCHARUM

ILEX RUGOSA

PINUS BUNGEANA

ILEX AQUIFOLIUM

ILEX OPACA

HEDRA HELIX CONGLOMERATAS

MALUS 'RED JADE'

BUXUS KOREAN

RHODODENDRON SAPPHIRE

R E S I D E N C E

GARAGE

RHODODENDRON BLACK BEAUTY

CORNUS FLORIDA

VINCA

RHODODENDRON RAMAPO

ILEX CRENATA MICROPHYLLA

ESPALIERED ILEX OPACA

BRICK PAVT

CHAMAECYPARIS OBTUSA NANA

ILEX AQUIFOLIUM CAMELLIAEFOLIUM

TAXUS BACCATA REPANDENS

ILEX CRENATA MICROPHYLLA

TSUGA CANADENSIS

ILEX AQUIFOLIUM

ILEX CRENATA

ILEX CRENATA

RHODODENDRON 'BLUE TIT'

RHODODENDRON 'VULCAN'

RHODODENDRON 'BOW BELLS'

MALUS 'MC INTOSH'

TAXUS BACCATA REPANDENS

HEDRA HELIX DELTOIDEA

KOELREUTERIA PANICULATA

PINUS STROBUS NANA

PACHISTIMA CANBYI

BUXUS MICROPHYLLA KOREANA

RHODODENDRON 'VULCAN'

ILEX OPACA

AZALEA FAIRY BELL & 'LOUISE GABLE'

ILEX AQUIPERNI BRILLANT

S I D E W A L K

0   5   10   20'

113

Treeform Japanese holly and a dwarf false-cypress make a fine green background for choice dwarf rhododendrons — 'Bow Bells', 'Blue Tit', and 'Blue Diamond'. These low-growing rhododendrons have excellent foliage all year and their flowers give a splash of color in May.

At each side of the steps on the lower terrace are old plants of English boxwood selected both for form and fragrance. Atlas cedar with its soft blue-green branches and the tall fragrant snowbell-tree, blooming in June, give height along the property line. A lacebark pine and 'Red Jade' crabapple accent the corner.

Part III

Garden Details

A garden is one aspect of your landscape design, perhaps the only part that you are interested in planning. Here are some ways to use plants in what we have come to think of as garden rooms. Even a little garden can be attractive right through the year if it is well designed and includes plants that will thrive under the conditions of your site. Lighting will increase your pleasure in your garden through summer evenings.

Garden sites

On small properties an evergreen garden set between the wings of a house or between house and property line is a possibility. A green garden can be successful in sunlight or shade, attractive summer and winter, and the plants may be chosen from a large group of beautiful evergreen shrubs. Viewed from the house, such a garden is a constant joy, especially in winter.

For early spring and late winter you can make a sunny spot into a "sun-catch," which is just what it sounds, a place that catches and holds sunshine for your pleasure and the early awakening of plants. If possible, face it southwest and protect it with a low sitting wall. Plant it with winter jasmine (*Jasminum nudiflorum*), winter hazel (*Corylopsis spicata*), winter honey-suckle (*Lonicera fragrantissima*), and early spring bulbs—species crocus, snowdrops, African iris perhaps. Such a garden will smell delicious and may be in bloom by late February.

Flower gardens, with sun most of the day, may be planned close to the house or at a little distance. You might incorporate yours with a terrace so that the two make one design. Here you can plant perennials alone or with bulbs or both with annuals.

Where there are many trees, you can plan a woodland garden. It can be formal or informal, perhaps with groups of azaleas and rhododendrons. Once the ground is cleared of tree roots, a garden in the woods has wonderful possibilities.

The city-dweller with limited outdoor space must be prepared to cope with smoke, soot, polluted air—and cats. However, if the soil is properly prepared at the outset, the challenges can be met and there is great joy in growing plants successfully under such difficulties.

Perhaps you want a garden for special plants—roses, iris, dahlias, or chrysanthemums. If space permits, you could have a series of garden rooms and let a favorite flower dominate each. Working out transition from one to another will give you a real opportunity for imaginative designing.

16.
Small Gardens and Garden Rooms

An Azalea Garden. This 18 x 30-foot garden between the porch and terrace of a colonial house is enclosed on the right with a low stone wall. In view from house and terrace above, it is always attractive with its simple pattern worked out with evergreens. A tall sorrel-tree selected for its narrow shape, fine foliage, and drooping panicles of white summer flowers casts a lovely shadow on the wall of the house. Below, long-stalked hollies with dangling red berries make a pleasing foreground for the high wall of the terrace. Low white azaleas, dwarf holly, and Japanese andromeda are planted along the walk. The central area, outlined with low hollies, includes double white tulips 'Mt. Tacoma' for spring followed by white begonias for summer and then white chrysanthemums for fall.

Tree

Oxydendrum arboreum	Sorrel-tree or sourwood

Shrubs

Azalea 'Delaware Valley White'	
Enkianthus campanulatus	Redvein enkianthus
Ilex crenata convexa	Boxleaf holly
Helleri	Heller or dwarf holly
rotunda	Roundleaf holly
pedunculosa	Longstalk holly
Pieris japonica	Japanese andromeda
floribunda	Dwarf andromeda

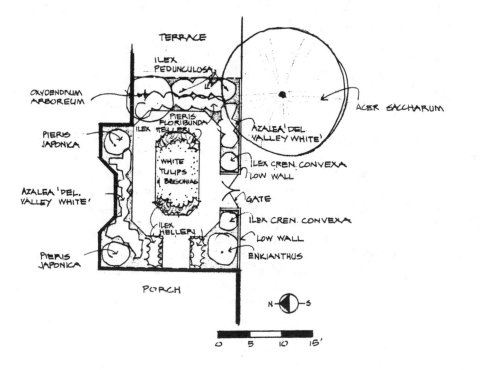

119

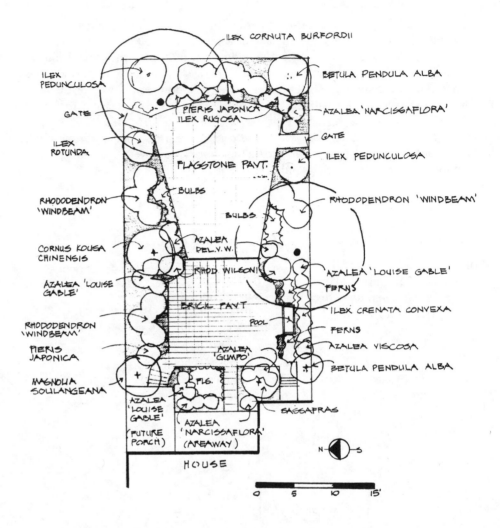

ILEX CORNUTA BURFORDII

ILEX PEDUNCULOSA

BETULA PENDULA ALBA

GATE

PIERIS JAPONICA
ILEX RUGOSA

AZALEA 'NARCISSAFLORA'

GATE

ILEX ROTUNDA

ILEX PEDUNCULOSA

FLAGSTONE PAVT.

BULBS

RHODODENDRON 'WINDBEAM'

BULBS

RHODODENDRON 'WINDBEAM'

CORNUS KOUSA CHINENSIS

AZALEA DEL.V.W.

RHOD WILSONI

AZALEA 'LOUISE GABLE'

AZALEA 'LOUISE GABLE'

FERNS

RHODODENDRON 'WINDBEAM'

BRICK PAVT

ILEX CRENATA CONVEXA

POOL

FERNS

PIERIS JAPONICA

AZALEA 'GUMPO'

AZALEA VISCOSA

MAGNOLIA SOULANGEANA

BETULA PENDULA ALBA

AZALEA 'LOUISE GABLE'

FIG.

(FUTURE PORCH)

AZALEA 'NARCISSAFLORA' (AREAWAY)

SASSAFRAS

N S

HOUSE

0   5   10   15'

A City Garden. A typical city backyard, only 25 x 50 feet and with two ailanthus trees, was used over the years as a playground for children. Now in keeping with the needs of a grown family it has been made into a garden. Because of differences in grade, two levels were developed; the smaller brick terrace close to the house is for dining and here (but not shown in the photograph) a tiny fountain drips water into an old painted iron sink. The larger upper terrace of flagstone includes the focal feature, a sculpture by John Rhoden.

Plants were selected for year-round interest and endurance of city conditions with very little sun. They included hollies, dwarf rhododendrons, a few deciduous azaleas. Trees are trimmed high to form a lacy ceiling over the garden. Bulbs add much to the spring picture; in summer, there are coral begonias and coral impatiens; in fall, containers of chysanthemums are brought in—a final bit of cheer for this city garden.

120

Trees

Ailanthus altissima	Tree-of-heaven
Betula pendula alba	White birch
Cornus Kousa chinensis	Chinese dogwood
Magnolia Souleangeana	Saucer magnolia
Sassafras albidum	Sassafras

Shrubs

Azalea 'Delaware Valley White'	
'Gumpo'	Dwarf white
'Louise Gable'	Pink
'Narcissiflora'	Yellow
viscosa	Swamp azalea
Ilex cornuta Burfordii	Burford holly
crenata convexa	Boxleaf holly
rotundifolia	Roundleaf holly
pedunculosa	Longstalk holly
Pieris japonica	Japanese andromeda
Rhododendron 'Windbeam'	Dwarf pale pink
Wilsonii	Dwarf lavender

Bulbs and perennials

The Pool Garden. Built on a ledge outside the living room, this rock-and-water garden features a series of pools. Water drips over stones to form shallow pools for birds and then splashes down to a larger pool below. Stone steps lead along the edge for the better view of hardy water-lilies and frogs, who arrived the day water was turned on. Rockcress, stonecrop, crested iris, tiarella, and other rock-garden plants grow under the old cedars.

122

Trees
   Cornus florida   Flowering dogwood
   Juniperus virginiana   Red-cedar

Shrubs
   Azalea Vaseyi   Pinkshell azalea
   Cotoneaster apiculata   Cranberry cotoneaster
   Rhododendron carolinianum   Carolina rhododendron

   Hardy water-lilies and rock-garden plants

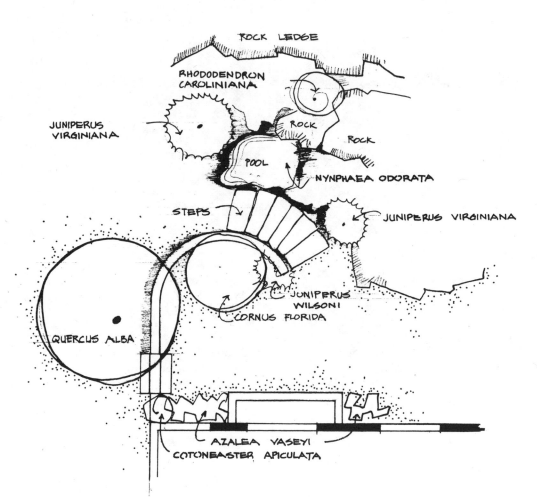

123

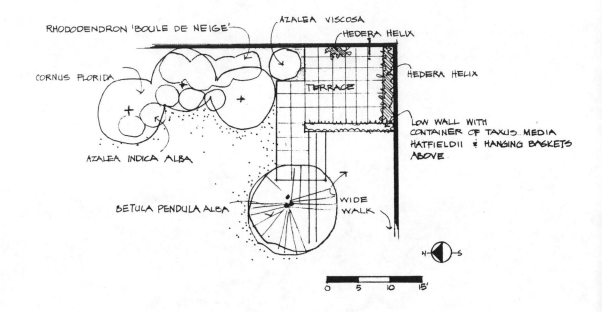

RHODODENDRON 'BOULE DE NEIGE'

AZALEA VISCOSA

HEDERA HELIX

CORNUS FLORIDA

HEDERA HELIX

TERRACE

LOW WALL WITH CONTAINER OF TAXUS MEDIA HATFIELDII & HANGING BASKETS ABOVE.

AZALEA INDICA ALBA

BETULA PENDULA ALBA

WIDE WALK

N — S

0   5   10   15'

Trees

Betula pendula alba	White birch
Cornus florida	Flowering dogwood

Shrubs

Azalea indica alba	White azalea
viscosa	Swamp azalea
Rhododendron 'Boule de Neige'	Dwarf white
Taxus media Hatfieldii	Hedge or Hatfield yew

Groundcover

Hedera Helix	English ivy

Basket plants

124

Sun-Catch. A corner, sunny and almost warm in winter and early spring, was paved to make a dining terrace. Tall flowering dogwoods and low white rhododendrons grow nearby. Hanging baskets of English ivy and geraniums and a plant-box of Hatfield yew screen the terrace from the entrance and give it privacy. BUHLE PHOTO

125

Enclosed Garden in Summer. Three walls of the house and a high brick wall surround this small garden which is in view of all the rooms. Therefore it was designed to be attractive through the year with emphasis on comfortable outdoor living and dining. Two circles of brick eliminate the need for grass. Wide borders include hollies and rhododendrons for winter interest, azaleas for spring, and roses for summer. Such a garden requires little maintenance and is a joy in all seasons.

In Winter. The dogwood in the corner and the Japanese andromeda and drooping leucothoe by the door look charming in the snow.

126

Trees

Cornus florida	Flowering dogwood
Sophora japonica	Japanese pagoda-tree

Shrubs

Azalea 'Gumpo'	Dwarf white
Buxus sempervirens suffruticosa	Dwarf or English boxwood
Ilex Aquifolium Aquiperni	Chinese holly
crenata 'Green Island'	Green Island holly
pedunculosa	Longstalk holly
Leucothoe axillaris	Dwarf leucothoe
Catesbaei	Drooping leucothoe
Pieris floribunda	Dwarf andromeda
japonica	Japanese andromeda
Rosa 'The Fairy'	Pink rose
Rhododendron 'Dora Amateis'	White
Wilsonii	Dwarf lavender
'Windbeam'	Dwarf pale pink
Viburnum Carlesii	Fragrant viburnum

Vines and groundcovers

Malus	Espaliered apple
Clematis paniculata	Sweet autumn clematis
Plumbago Larpentiae	Leadwort
Vinca minor	Myrtle or periwinkle

Potted plants, bulbs, and herbs

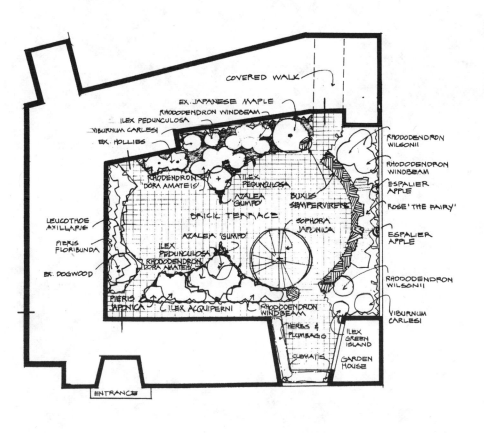

Town House Garden. This small terrace and garden at the rear of a 50 x 100-foot plot have given pleasure over many years. On the wide overhang the spring-blooming, pink mountain clematis grows luxuriantly, and is trimmed along the gutter line. A central panel of grass with surrounding beds forms the garden. At the opening to it, boxwood encloses six hybrid tea roses. On the left, the 3-foot rectangular bed is filled with pink tulips, 'Rosy Wings' and 'Sweet Harmony' and later, for summer bloom, with pink petunias 'Maytime'. On the right, an apple tree shades a border of hollies and viburnums selected to attract birds. Owner designed.

GOTTSCHO-SCHLEISNER PHOTO

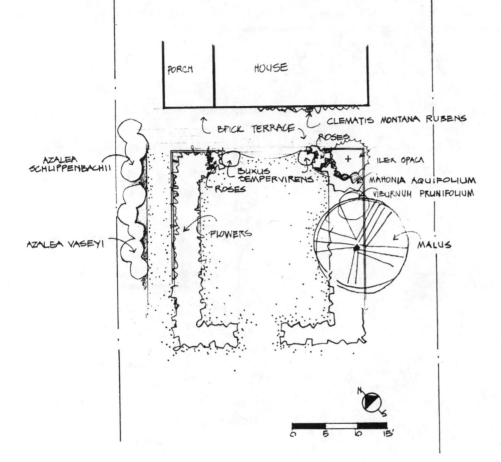

Trees

Ilex opaca   America holly
Malus   Apple

Shrubs

Azalea Schlippenbachii   Royal azalea
          Vaseyi   Pinkshell azalea
Buxus sempervirens   American box
Mahonia Aquifolium   Holly mahonia
Viburnum prunifolium   Blackhaw

Vines

Clematis montana rubens   Mountain clematis

Roses, bulbs, annuals

129

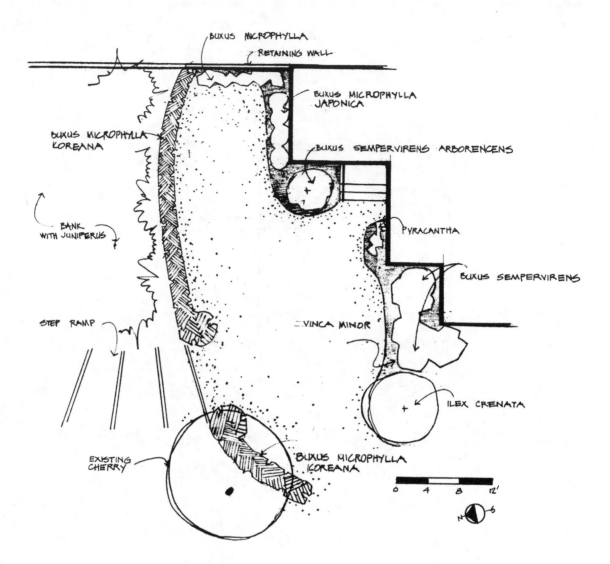

Shrubs

Buxus microphylla   Dwarf box
  japonica   Japanese dwarf box
  koreana   Korean box
  sempervirens   American box
  arborescens   Tree box
Illex crenata   Japanese holly

Vines

Pyracantha coccinea Lalandii   Firethorn
Vinca minor   Myrtle or periwinkle

130

Garden of Boxwood. This evergreen, usually associated with a pattern garden is planted here on the only level area there was near this house on Cape Cod. The sheltered area beyond the door serves as green garden and terrace, a delightful place from which to view the distant ocean. The scent of box and the different characteristics of the five varieties make this a most interesting evergreen garden, pleasant in all seasons.

At the right, the tall tree box is effective with its graceful feathery foliage. Specimen English box is planted next to the house. At the left, around the corner below windows, Japanese dwarf box stays in scale; along the retaining wall, the tiny dwarf box grows high enough for delineation but stays low enough not to interfere with a view of the woods. Korean box makes a hedge at the top of the bank. For winter protection, plants are sprayed in late fall and then again in March with an anti-desiccant. All have proved hardy through recent winters. CROSSLEY PHOTO

Aconitum Fischeri	Monkshood
Anthemis nobilis 'Moonlight'	Camomile
Aquilegia Hybrids	Columbine
Artemisia 'Silver King'	Sagebrush or wormwood
Aster 'Harrington's Pink'	Hardy aster
Astilbe 'Peach Blossom'	
Chrysanthemum 'Yellow Spoon'	
'Betty'	Pink
Delphinium chinensis	Chinese larkspur
Hybrids	Tall delphinium
Dianthus plumarius 'Her Majesty'	White cottage pink
Dictamnus albus	Gasplant
Digitalis Mertonensis	Foxglove
Hemerocallis 'Lemona'	Day-lily
Heuchera sanguinea	Coralbells
Iberis sempervirens	Candytuft
Iris germanica 'Gudrun'	German iris
Kaempferi 'Albatross'	Japanese iris
Lilium candidum	Madonna lily
Mertensia virginica	Virginia bluebells
Oenothera fruticosa Youngii	Evening primrose
Paeonia 'Le Cygne'	White peony
'Philippe Rivoire'	Crimson
'Sarah Bernhardt'	Pink
Papaver orientale 'Mrs. Perry'	Salmon Oriental poppy
'Perry's White'	
Phlox 'Mrs. Jenkins'	White
Pyrethrum 'Helen'	Painted daisy

132

A Perennial Garden. This oval design includes a terrace and four beds, three planted with sun-loving perennials, the fourth under the old apple tree with shade-tolerant plants. To facilitate maintenance a grass path circles the outside of the beds. Such a garden is a source of pleasure for many months and perennials, once they are established, require little attention compared to annuals. The same rules that apply to designing a property apply to designing flower gardens—plants are chosen for foliage, form, color, and time of bloom with low edging plants, tall background plants, and in-between filler plants. It helps to work out details on a ¼-inch scale plan. Then keep your plan as a record for future reference. BUHLE PHOTO

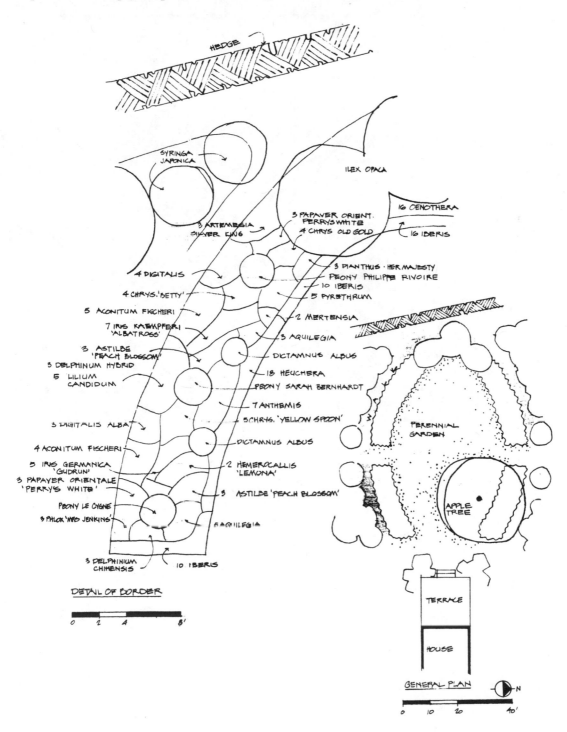

HEDGE

SYRINGA JAPONICA

ILEX OPACA

16 OENOTHERA

3 PAPAVER ORIENT. PERRYS WHITE
4 CHRYS OLD GOLD

16 IBERIS

3 ARTEMESIA SILVER KING

3 DIANTHUS · HER MAJESTY
PEONY PHILIPPE RIVOIRE
10 IBERIS
5 PYRETHRUM

4 DIGITALIS

4 CHRYS. 'BETTY'

5 ACONITUM FISCHERI

7 IRIS KAEMPFERI 'ALBATROSS'

2 MERTENSIA

3 AQUILEGIA

3 ASTILBE 'PEACH BLOSSOM'

DICTAMNUS ALBUS

3 DELPHINUM HYBRID

18 HEUCHERA

5 LILIUM CANDIDUM

PEONY SARAH BERNHARDT

7 ANTHEMIS

5 CHRYS. 'YELLOW SPOON'

3 DIGITALIS ALBA

DICTAMNUS ALBUS

4 ACONITUM FISCHERI

2 HEMEROCALLIS 'LEMONA'

5 IRIS GERMANICA 'GUDRUN'

3 PAPAVER ORIENTALE 'PERRY'S WHITE'

3 ASTILBE 'PEACH BLOSSOM'

PEONY LE CYGNE

3 PHLOX 'MRS JENKINS'

5 AQUILEGIA

3 DELPHINIUM CHINENSIS

10 IBERIS

PERENNIAL GARDEN

APPLE TREE

DETAIL OF BORDER

0   2   4   8'

TERRACE

HOUSE

GENERAL PLAN   N

0   10   20   40'

A feature for your garden is usually one of the final decisions in your landscape planning. Whether it is to be a simple birdbath of hollowed stone or a handsome gazebo on a hill, a well-designed garden gate, a woodland pool, or bridge, it will be a vital accent. Try to place your feature either as focal point or as incidental accent where you wish to draw attention. If a handsome plant is to be the feature, select one that will be in sharp contrast to the shape, height, and texture of nearby plants. Perhaps a gnarled old tree or an unusual evergreen already on the property can serve. For a small place where a garden is in close association, a house wall could be ornamented with a wall fountain and potted plants in attractive containers grouped below. All features need not be immediate eye-catchers. Some may be hidden and at a distance from the house; a path might lead to a reflecting pool deep in the woods.

Ideas for garden features

Garden gate: Plant identical specimens on each side, as a pair of yews or box.

Bench: Place it beneath a flowering tree or give it a background of yew.

Bridge: If you have a stream, put a simple board bridge across it or if it is shallow, a line of big stepping stones.

Pool, fountain, or water drip: Remember that the sound as well as the sight of water is refreshing. Use a round pool as a central feature, perhaps with a re-circulating pump, or an informal pool placed below a rock ledge, or pipe in water to drip over stones.

Birdbath and feeder: Place these near the house in easy reach for refilling and where you can observe the birds from a window. An evergreen or well-branched tree nearby can serve for sanctuary and "drying room."

Garden sculpture: Choose a good piece, not just anything, and set it off with a foliage background of contrasting color.

Sundial: Place this in an open space at the end of a path or intersection.

Wellhead: Set this in a paved area with a tall overhanging tree.

Gazebo: Build this for a delightful feature in the woods or on a hill with a view.

Containers: Select these with restraint; unusual pots and urns can add a great deal to the garden picture but there should not be too many kinds used in any one place.

A plant or group of plants: Choose a spectacular specimen or several plants to accent some element in your design.

17.
Garden
Features

Garden Gate. Plain concrete piers with decorated stone baskets serve as pillars for a wrought-iron gate and make a handsome entrance to a garden. An adjoining fence is not required; hybrid lilacs are used in a hedge at the sides. BUHLE PHOTO

Bridge in a Wild Garden. A simple 5-foot bridge of 6-inch boards highlights this area of the brook, and leads to a wild-flower garden in which are grown many dwarf rhododendrons and azaleas. Daffodils are planted for early spring effect. Good for naturalizing are: 'February Gold', 'Carlton', 'Mrs. Krelage', 'Rembrandt', 'Tinker', 'Actea', 'Beersheba', and 'Fortune'. Thriving here in semishade are alders, pinxterbloom, and sweet pepperbush. These grow along the edge of the stream among masses of trillium, white snakeroot (*Eupatorium rugosum*) Solomon's-seal (*Polygonatum*), bluebells (*Mertensia*), and primroses; in fall autumn crocus and colchicum appear. Owner designed

136

Bench and Sculpture. A garden bench made from a heavy piece of oakwood balanced on sewer-pipe sections filled with sand, a birdbath in an oversized saucer on a tree stump, and terra-cotta birds by the sculptor, Dorothy Riester, make Helen Van Pelt Wilson's small round garden all the more interesting and delightful. A fringe-tree shades the bench. The circle, outlined by laurel and lilies is filled in with plants of easy maintenance—Jacob's-ladder (*Polemonium reptans*), plantain-lilies, and Christmas ferns. Rhoda Tarantino design

Sculpture. A charming little lead figure holds a birdbath in a planting opposite a terrace; white *Azalea indica alba* and inkberry (*Ilex glabra*), dwarf English box (*Buxus sempervirens suffruticosa*), and low holly (*Ilex crenata Helleri*) constitute a planting that is in good scale and always attractive.

Bench and Urns. A wrought-iro bench with old iron urns deco rates a small paved city garde where white birches and whi picket fence repeat the white the bench.

Sculpture. Outside the kitchen window a large porcelain cat watches over this little terrace surrounded by evergreen shrubs. The planting of year-round green includes boxleaf holly, evergreen barberry, a handsome espaliered pyracantha on the wall, and an ivy groundcover with pots of geraniums for summer color. Owner designed

Water Feature. Water for birds and also for five pet dogs was a requirement for a feature in this little garden. Water from the upper shell for the birds drips into the lower basin where large stones provide a good place for dogs to stand without disturbance to ground planting. In the background, there are low white azaleas and a star magnolia with overhanging branches, a perch for birds.

Pool. In the corner of a wall at the edge of a grass terrace a bronze duck sprays water into a 3 x 5-foot plastic pool. The pool with a re-circulating pump can be filled by a garden hose. Flat field stones hide the plastic edge and the planting is changed three times during the growing season. In spring there are white tulips and blue forget-me-nots, then pink and yellow lantanas; in fall, *Chrysanthemum* 'Betty' is a cloud of pink. Through winter, leucothoe with its drooping bronze foliage makes an attractive evergreen setting. BUHLE PHOTO

A woodland path of pine bark leads to a gazebo at the top of the hill. Yellow *Azalea mollis,* 'Narcissiflora', and Knap Hill Yellow with white *A. indica alba* and 'Palestrina' grow well with the Japanese andromeda. As a groundcover among the existing oaks and dogwoods, ferns—Christmas, cinnamon, lady, New York, and ostrich—are interplanted with galax, shortia, lamium, Mayapple, dwarf iris, foam-flowers, liriope, and day-lilies. Owner designed

Reflecting Pool. This shallow pool with wide grass banks makes a lovely setting for a garden designed by the owner. The surrounding woods of tall trees are underplanted with dogwood and masses of white azaleas—*Azalea indica alba,* 'Delaware Valley White', 'Palestrina', 'Polaris', and 'Rose Greeley'—and choice rhododendrons with various groundcovers providing a long season of bloom and a contrast of textures.

A waterfall cascading into a pool made from a cement-mixing trough is an attractive feature at the edge of the woods and opposite living-room windows. Leucothoe, white Exbury azaleas, andromeda, and Carolina rhododendrons surround the area with ferns and puschkinia and *Iris Danfordiae* for March; *Scilla siberica* 'Spring Beauty' and *Narcissus* 'Beersheba', 'Actea', and 'Mount Hood' for April; and for May, *Frittileria, Scilla campanulata,* and *Narcissus* 'Cheerfulness' and 'Thalia'. Owner designed

Groundcovers are a key to leisure gardening. Once established they save you hours of work. However, at the start before growth thickens, keep plants free of weeds, well fed, and well watered. In time, a well-chosen groundcover pretty much takes care of itself. Difficult shady corners and under-tree areas are the first places you are apt to plant groundcovers, but there are many other situations where the right creeping plant offers a practical solution, preventing erosion and giving interest through the year.

In front of your house an evergreen groundcover of myrtle or pachysandra will tie your plants together, relate them to the ground, and make a green carpet at your entrance. You can plant banks too steep for mowing with one of the fragrant trailers. Hall's honeysuckle quickly covers a steep slope but it is terribly invasive and can become a nuisance unless there is plenty of room for it to roam. The fragrant Memorial rose, *Rosa Wichuraiana* and 'Evergreen Gem', both white, 'Coral Creeper' and pink 'Max Graf' offer spectacular bloom. *Rosa rugosa repens alba,* the dwarf white rugosa rose, is tolerant of sandy soil and salt spray.

A good evergreen groundcover for a sunny, sandy hillside is the bearberry *Arctostaphylos uva-ursi* which grows wild in many parts of Long Island but is also available at nurseries. It is somewhat difficult to get started but once established makes a close mat for a steep bank. Then there are such evergreens as the Wilton and Sargent junipers, also the native *Juniperus horizontalis.*

The low-growing euonymus and the various English ivies thrive under trees. The lovely old-fashioned lily-of-the-valley with its wonderful fragrance is particularly nice under lilacs. The leaves alone are attractive but for flowers good light is essential. For a groundcover in a woodsy area there are ferns, violets, partridge-berry, and epimedium in white, yellow, lilac, and red. These all stand shade and associate well with the taller woodland plants.

To make a very sunny area stay carefree yet look like a garden, plant groundcovers with worthwhile bloom—ajuga, veronica, nepeta, thyme, and sedum. Three unusual groundcovers that grow to 2 feet or more in the sun are yellowroot (*Zanthorhiza*), bottlebush (*Aesculus parviflora*), and flowering locust or rose acacia (*Robinia hispida*).

Then there are the pretty little low plants to set between paving and terrace stones—rockcress, thyme, thrift, pearlwort, mint, and others.

Planting and spacing

To get your groundcovers to grow quickly, dig holes at least twice as wide as the pot or roots and fill in with a mixture of peatmoss or humus and good soil. Spacing varies with different plants. Set small kinds like woodruff 9 to 12 inches apart. Give tall rampant growers like rose acacia 3 feet each. Stagger plants to obtain uniform coverage. Once plants start to grow, fasten down the runners with long hairpins.

18.
Groundcovers and Paving Plants

143

Dependable evergreen groundcovers

Vinca minor, myrtle or periwinkle, creeping, vinelike, with bright blue spring flowers for sun or shade is one of the best when established. It forms dense mats yet early bulbs—grape hyacinths, scillas, and narcissus—will thrive when interplanted if they are fertilized every year. *Bowlesii,* known as Bowles Variety, is superior with larger flowers but plants are slower to establish. There are also white and purple forms and some doubles. Use the white kind in a little corner where it will be noticed.

Pachysandra terminalis, Japanese pachysandra or spurge, one of the most used and satisfactory groundcovers, grows 6 to 10 inches tall with inconspicuous white flower spikes in early spring; it prefers shade and acid soil and spreads by underground runners. The American species, *Pachysandra procumbens,* is less attractive.

Hedera Helix, English ivy is especially good in shade, burns in winter sun; *baltica* is an excellent small-leaved form that holds its winter color better and is a more controlled grower. New cultivars '238th Street', 'Buttercup', and 'Stardust' are worth trying if you have the room.

For shade

Asperula odorata, sweet woodruff, a pretty 8-inch perennial, with small white flowers in May, spreads rapidly; leaves are used in May wine.

Galax aphylla, a 10-inch evergreen with bronzy heart-shaped leaves and spikes of white June flowers spreads slowly, and is most effective.

Euonymus Fortunei (*E. radicans*), wintercreeper is a hardy evergreen that soon covers large areas with shiny foliage. A number of cultivars are available.

Shrubs for sun

Cotoneaster Dammeri, bearberry cotoneaster, a prostrate evergreen with rooting stems bears white flowers followed by bright red berries that last into winter. Also good for sunny places are *C. horizontalis* and *C. microphylla thymifolia,* both to 3 feet.

Calluna vulgaris, wild Scotch heather is a long-blooming, low bushy plant with rosy-lavender flowers from July to September. The 3-inch cultivar, 'Mrs. R. H. Gray', forms broad dense green mats with lavender flowers in July and August. All heathers are evergreen and decorative throughout the year. The heaths, *Erica carnea,* are equally good and bloom in spring.

Juniperus chinensis Sargentii, Sargent juniper, a low spreading evergreen, has excellent winter color and it will grow downward, an advantage in many situations. 'Bar Harbor' makes a dense quick-growing mat with steel-blue foliage.

Forsythia 'Arnold Dwarf' is low and quick-growing with excellent foliage; bloom is not showy.

144

"Gardenesque" groundcovers

Epimedium, a perennial with heart-shaped leaves, grows 6 to 12 inches, depending on the cultivar selected, and is covered in May and June with delicate yellow, white, pink, or red flowers; very fine for partial shade or sun.

Pachistima Canbyi is a compact, evergreen shrub spreading to 18 inches but less than 1 foot high with dark green leaves and inconspicuous flowers; for sun or light shade.

Plumbago Larpentiae, leadwort, a spreading perennial to 8 inches appears late in spring and is covered with bright blue flowers from July to November; for sun or semishade.

Myosotis scorpioides (*M. palustris*), forget-me-not, a fast-growing 8-inch perennial with light green foliage and blue spring flowers, is easy to grow from seed; for light, open shade.

Most useful ferns

Dennstaedtia punctilobula, hay-scented fern, is yellow-green with the aroma of hay in sun or when dried; turns light rust color in fall; a rampant grower to 2 feet in somewhat damp open shade; deciduous.

Dryopteris spinulosa, toothed or common wood fern, is for moist, slightly acid locations in open shade; grows to 30 inches; nearly evergreen.

Osmunda cinnamomea, cinnamon fern, is the showiest fiddlehead; lovely with *Pieris japonica* and day-lilies; grows to 3 feet; deciduous.

Osmunda regalis, royal fern, is lovely and graceful for banks and paths with Japanese iris; needs a damp, highly acid location; grows to 4 feet; deciduous.

Polystichum acrostichoides, Christmas fern, is fine for the edge of woodland and interplanted with narcissus, 2 feet, almost evergreen.

Thelypteris noveboracensis, New York fern, yellow-green to medium green, makes a nice contrast to the darker green of many other ferns; needs rich moist, slightly acid loam, a rapid spreader, deciduous.

For the seashore in sun

Arctostaphylos uva-ursi, bearberry, a dense creeping evergreen, covers large areas; its small leathery leaves and white spring flower bells are followed by red berries that last all winter.

Cytisus decumbens, ground-broom, is evergreen with quantities of bright yellow flowers in April and May.

Leiophyllum buxifolium, box sand-myrtle, makes 2-foot evergreen mounds spreading slowly over sandy areas; white fluffy flowers in June.

Rosa rugosa repens alba, dwarf rugosa rose, forms a hardy carpet for sandy sunny banks; white June flowers are followed by red seed hips; tolerates salt spray.

For steep banks

Lonicera japonica Halliana, Hall's honeysuckle, is fast-growing, strong, invasive in sun or shade; almost impossible to control but excellent on large banks where no other plant will interrupt its luxurious growth; fragrant flowers all summer; can be mowed once a year; almost evergreen.

Rosa Wichuraiana, Memorial rose, is dark green and prickly with lovely fragrant white flowers; excellent for large sunny areas. The hybrid 'Max Graf' has large pink flowers. 'Evergreen Gem' and 'Coral Creeper' are other fine trailing roses; almost evergreen.

Hypericum calycinum, St. John's-wort, grows to 1 foot with yellow midsummer flowers.

Xanthorhiza simplicissima, yellowroot, forms 12 to 16-inch bushes spreading by underground roots to make dense cover in a short time in damp shady places; inconspicuous flowers; deciduous.

Weedy covers that can be pests

Nepeta hederacea, ground ivy or Gill-over-the-ground, is a tiny purple-flowering creeper with scalloped leaves; deciduous.

Aegopodium Podagraria, goutweed or bishops-weed, grows 6 to 12 inches high all green or with green-and-white leaves and white flowers; deciduous; spreads by underground runners.

Lysimachia Nummularia, moneywort or creeping Jennie, opens bright yellow summer flowers; deciduous.

Polygonum Reynowtria, dwarf polygonum, knotweed or fleece-flower, is strong and fast, and like the others can become a pest; foliage turns red in fall with feathery pink sprays of flowers.

Paving plants for walks and terraces

Arabis procurrens	Creeping rockcress, white flowers, early spring
Cerastium tomentosum	Snow-in-summer, white flowers, early summer
Chrysogonum	Golden-star, yellow flowers, summer
Mazus reptans	Lavender flowers, summer
Mentha Requienii	Creeping mint, tiny white flowers and leaves
Thymus Serpyllum	Creeping thyme, lilac bloom
albus	White
'Annie Hall'	Light pink

Along a walk Pickwick crocus grows well in a groundcover of myrtle. The shiny leaves of the vine and bright blue flowers of the bulbs in May are set off by the background of hollies.

Myrtle planted among cotoneasters and junipers makes an excellent year-round groundcover at each side of the entrance steps.

Beside this doorway pachysandra grows under a clump of birch with early scillas interplanted. Every year they are a mass of blue in May along with the white flowers of pachysandra. Ivy fills the narrow beds along the foundation of the house and is being trained up the wall.

Lily-of-the-valley grows on a bank among rocks beside railroad-tie steps and offers pleasant fragrance along this walk to the mailbox.

148

Heaths and heathers thrive on this hillside at the service end of the house where great boulders were placed to make planting pockets in the somewhat acid sandy soil with good drainage. There is a long colorful season from the spring heath, *Erica carnea,* which blooms from February to April, to the late fall heathers, *Calluna vulgaris.* The pink 'Mrs. H. E. Beale' and 'Mrs. R. H. Gray' are two of the best. Dwarf mugho pines, low junipers, and low hollies enhance the planting. Multiple-stemmed dogwoods and mountain-laurel at the top of the bank conceal a drying yard.

'Bar Harbor' junipers at the edge of the pool soften the line between flagstone and grass. Yews outline the top of a wall, which the climbing hydrangea is covering. Funkia and goutweed grow at the base. At the right, 'Hyperion' day-lilies give a splash of color for weeks during the summer. Such planting keeps maintenance to a minimum.

In a woodland planting foam-flower, *Tiarella cordifolia,* and false Solomon's-seal. *Smilacina racemosa,* make a carpet under tall trees.

Between driveway and house and beneath a dogwood tree the New York fern, *Thelypteris noveboracensis,* rises from a bed of pachysandra, giving a lovely feathery effect through the summer months while the pachysandra stays green through winter.

Beneath the white blossoms of the crabapple 'Katherine' are masses of ferns, Jacobs-ladder, and *Phlox divaricata*. The phlox is allowed to self-sow so new plants develop in quantity beneath the ferns.

In a low raised bed along a walk to the vegetable garden, a groundcover of strawberries is attractive in flower and leaf and bears excellent fruit. The wild French strawberry 'Fraises des Bois' is also a fine everbearing border plant.

151

19.
Hedges and Concealments

Today a hedge has more uses than to hide something, as laundry yard or compost pile, although this is still one of its functions. A hedge can also be part of the planting design whether outlining a formal entrance court, running as a dark green band below a window, or forming a background for a flower garden. Hedges recently have become more important because contemporary architecture requires plants of definite form that naturally stay low or can be kept in proper proportion with some trimming. A hedge may be evergreen or deciduous, sheared or unsheared, as low as a foot for edging, as high as 15 feet for screening.

Select hedge material that suits existing conditions of sun, shade, wind, low ground, sandy soil, or a hilly site, something likely to be free of disease and insects. Above all it must be hardy in your area; a hedge that does not thrive is unsightly. Consider whether you want evergreen or deciduous material with foliage coarse or fine. A hedge of holly shines all winter and gives a feeling of lightness to a planting.

Planting and trimming

For proper growth, hedges require good soil and proper spacing. This varies according to what you select. Space low hedge plants 1 foot apart; those of medium height, like some yews, 2 feet apart; tall hemlocks require 4 feet. Most hedge plants look better in single rather than double rows. When planted this way, they are easier to trim and provide a better ending to the row.

All hedges require trimming to keep them healthy. Some require more than others. The time to trim is after new growth starts, usually late in June. It is important to start the clipping as soon as your new hedge starts to grow so that it will get dense; if you wait until your hedge has reached the height you need, you will find it unsightly and thin. *Always keep the base somewhat wider than the top.* This practice allows sun to reach the lower part and forces thicker growth there, thus avoiding bare stems. Also, a narrow top holds less snow, a hazard that weighs down branches and can break them. If snow does collect, try to shake it off as soon as possible, especially from evergreen hedges.

Hedges for special uses

Some plants grow naturally into narrow upright forms as the Hatfield yew, *Taxus media Hatfieldii,* which needs only occasional trimming. Use it for narrow strips beside a garage or as background for a flower border. A deciduous plant for either purpose might be the winged *Euonymus alatus compactus,* which stands shearing and has colorful autumn foliage.

When you need a hedge for a barrier to hide an unsightly view or to conceal a road, select material that grows tall and wide, if it is to go unsheared, and allow 6 to 7 feet for each plant. Set plants well within your boundary

152

to keep your hedge from encroaching on your neighbor's property. Buckthorn, *Rhamnus cathartica,* with short spines at the tips of branches, makes a strong hardy hedge. The wayfaring-tree, *Viburnum Lantana,* is also vigorous, endures part shade, and bears white flowers followed by red fruit.

For a garden background, select hedge material without invasive roots that will interfere with flowering plants closeby. Japanese holly, *Ilex crenata,* is excellent while privet roots are always greedy. To control them, sink a strip of sheet metal beside them to a 3-foot depth. Regel privet, *Ligustrum obtusifolium Regelianum,* grows to about 6 feet and may be sheared or let grow naturally. The black berries are a favorite of pheasants.

For a windbreak, you want a thick twiggy grower. Arbor-vitae can stand snow and wind and would be good for a Vermont hillside. In a windswept Long Island field, plant blueberries, *Vaccinium pensylvanicum,* with pointed leaf buds, bright red autumn color, and fruit attractive to birds.

For the seashore, select plants that can stand salt spray and wind as bayberry (*Myrica pensylvanica*), beach plum (*Prunus maritima*), or Japanese black pine (*Pinus Thunbergii*). Privet, *Ligustrum,* grows exceptionally well at the shore and, unsheared, makes a fine billowing outline.

For flowering material in light shade use mountain-laurel, *Kalmia latifolia;* in sun, one of the shrub roses, *Rosa rugosa* or *R. multiflora,* both rampant growers. For a low planting, there is *Abelia grandiflora* blooming from July to frost. The yews (*Taxus*), inkberry (*Ilex glabra*), and blackhaw (*Viburnum prunifolium*), are good for planting in the shade of great old trees.

The lowest-growing hedge, really an edging, is used along a walk or a flower garden. For this purpose two are excellent: dwarf English box, *Buxus sempervirens suffruticosa,* and germander, *Teucrium Chamaedrys,* a woody plant with small evergreen leaves and thick dense growth that may be sheared before it blooms if you do not care for the purple flowers.

Of course, there are situations and designs where hedges or other plantings cannot be used as concealments. Then consider a fence or wall. Select a material for either in keeping with the buildings on your property and the general style of your place.

On the outside, the yews associate well with hemlocks, Japanese holly, and *Rhododendron* 'Betty Hume'. A multiple-stemmed honey-locust shades terrace and living room.

To conceal a road from the living room but keep open a view of the lake, Japanese yews, *Taxus cuspidata,* which need trimming only once a year, have been planted in 24 x 30-inch wooden containers built along the edge of the terrace. The lake is clearly seen above the dark mass of yew foliage.

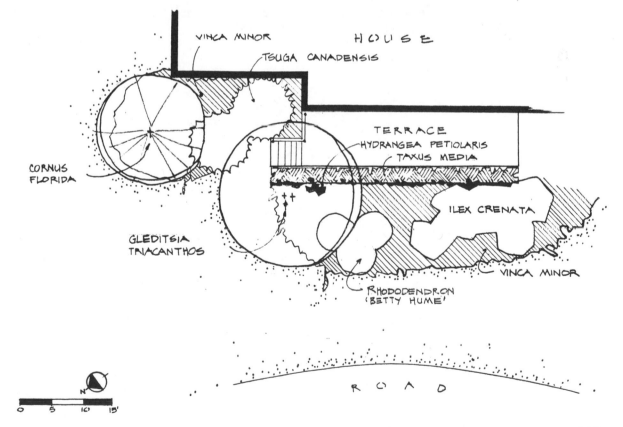

VINCA MINOR   H O U S E

TSUGA CANADENSIS

CORNUS
FLORIDA

TERRACE
HYDRANGEA PETIOLARIS
TAXUS MEDIA

ILEX CRENATA

GLEDITSIA
TRIACANTHOS

VINCA MINOR

RHODODENDRON
'BETTY HUME'

N

0   5   10   15'

R O A D

155

Dwarf black yews, *Taxus cuspidata nigra,* will eventually grow together at the top of this retaining wall and form there an interesting green outline above the terrace. The hedge will also serve as a windbreak.

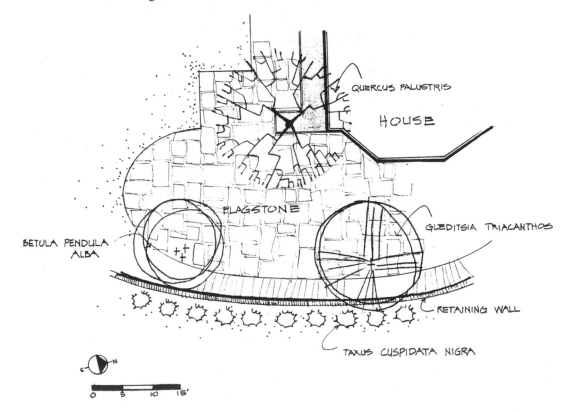

QUERCUS PALUSTRIS

HOUSE

FLAGSTONE

BETULA PENDULA ALBA

GLEDITSIA TRIACANTHOS

RETAINING WALL

TAXUS CUSPIDATA NIGRA

0   5   10   15'

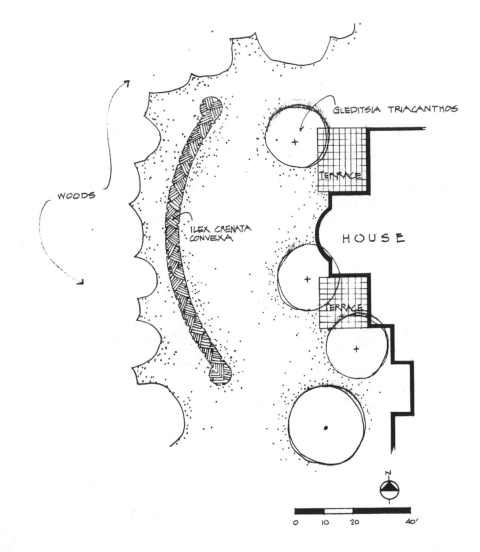

GLEDITSIA TRIACANTHOS

WOODS

ILEX CRENATA
CONVEXA

TERRACE

H O U S E

TERRACE

N

0   10   20   40'

This hedge breaks the line between lawn and woods making a nice demarcation between the formal outdoor living area and the natural growth of the hillside. The low evergreen boxleaf holly, *Ilex crenata convexa,* always looks neat yet needs pruning only once during the growing season.

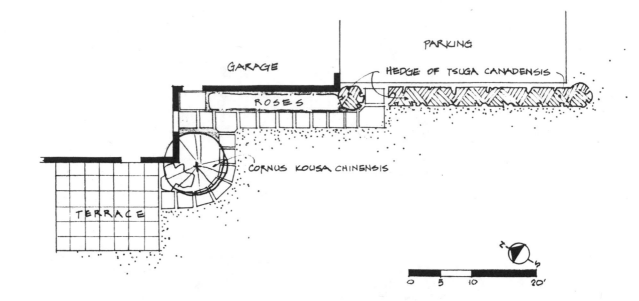

GARAGE

PARKING

HEDGE OF TSUGA CANADENSIS

ROSES

CORNUS KOUSA CHINENSIS

TERRACE

0 5 10 20'

At the right, a hedge of Canada hemlock, *Tsuga canadensis,* hides the garage court. Its graceful form, light texture, good green color, and adaptability make it useful for many situations. Hemlock stands severe pruning or can be allowed to grow naturally; it thrives in sun, also in shade if well fed.

Here concealment of a busy service yard is achieved with a redwood fence adorned with a white wisteria. Perennial candytuft, *Iberis sempervirens,* edges the bed of tree peonies, *Paeonia suffruticosa.* In this corner the picture is lovely in spring when all are in bloom and the place is pleasing the rest of the year with contrasting textures of foliage. Clara Coffey, L.A.

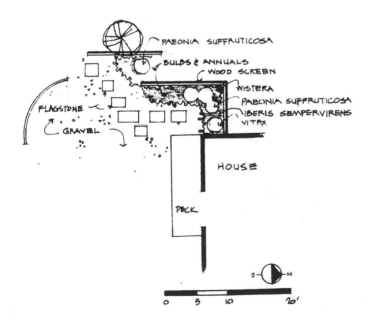

159

To outline a parking area, plants of Japanese holly, *Ilex crenata,* were set 4 feet apart. It took several years for them to grow together into this dense hedge, now 2-feet wide and 4-feet tall. It is trimmed in July and again lightly in September.

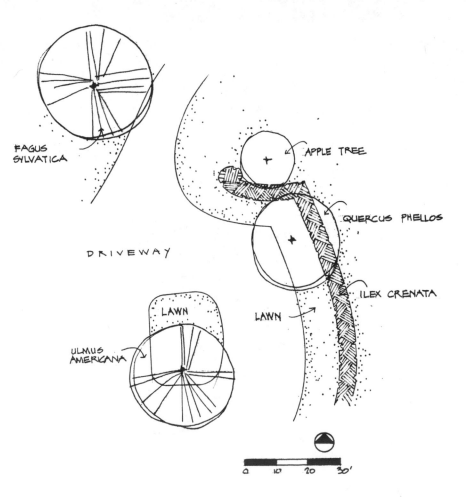

FAGUS SYLVATICA

APPLE TREE

QUERCUS PHELLOS

DRIVEWAY

ILEX CRENATA

LAWN

LAWN

ULMUS AMERICANA

0   10   20   30'

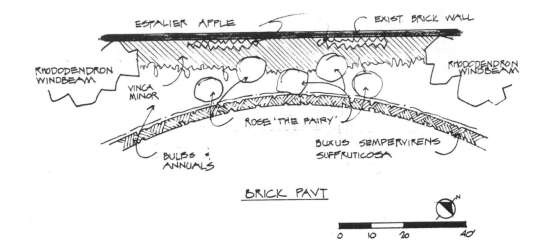

ESPALIER APPLE   EXIST BRICK WALL

RHODODENDRON WINDBEAM

VINCA MINOR

ROSE 'THE FAIRY'

RHODODENDRON WINDBEAM

BUXUS SEMPERVIRENS SUFFRUTICOSA

BULBS & ANNUALS

BRICK PAVT

0   10   20   40'

N

To make a wall pattern espaliered fruit trees are delightful and these can be purchased in a number of forms. Here apple trees against a brick wall bear good fruit. In front, a bed of daffodils is outlined with dwarf box.

161

Under a window where the overhang is not too wide just one kind of plant looks best. Here *Leucothoe axillaris* grows well. With only an occasional pruning, it can be kept below the height of the window sill.

SELECTED HEDGE PLANTS

Botanical Name	Common Name	Values	Height in Feet
Abelia grandiflora	Glossy abelia	Long-blooming	3
Buxus sempervirens suffruticosa	Dwarf English box	Sheared for formality	2
Euonymus alatus compactus	Winged euonymus	Colorful fall foliage	4
Iberis sempervirens	Perennial candytuft	Edging evergreen	1
Ilex crenata	Japanese holly	Garden background	4
convexa	Boxleaf holly	One yearly pruning	2
glabra	Inkberry or winterberry	For shade	3
Kalmia latifolia	Mountain-laurel	Light shade	5
Leucothoe axillaris	Dwarf leucothoe	Light shade	3
Ligustrum obtusifolium Regelianum	Regel privet	Shear or not; seashore	6
Myrica pensylvanica	Bayberry	Seashore	5
Pinus Thunbergii	Japanese black pine	Seashore	
Prunus maritima	Beach plum	Seashore	4
Rhamnus cathartica	Buckthorn	Strong and spiny	7
Rosa multiflora	Shrub rose	Rampant and thorny	
rugosa	Shrub rose		3
Taxus cuspidata	Japanese yew	Yearly pruning	3
nana	Dwarf Japanese yew	Edging	2
media Hatfieldii	Hedge or Hatfield yew	For narrow strips	5
Teucrium Chamaedrys	Germander	Edging evergreen	1
Thuja occidentalis	American Arbor-vitae	Stands snow, wind	6
Tsuga canadensis	Canada hemlock	Sun or shade	6
Viburnum Lantana	Wayfaring-tree	Red fruit, shade	5
prunifolium	Blackhaw	Shade	5
Vaccinium pensylvanicum	Blueberry	Wind, fall color, fruit	5

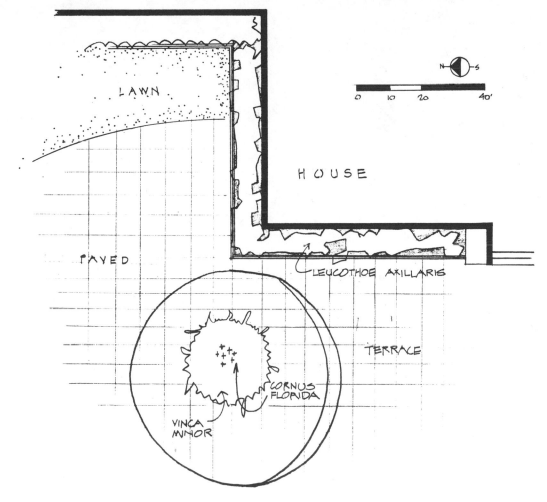

LAWN

HOUSE

N

0   10   20   40'

PAVED

LEUCOTHOE AXILLARIS

TERRACE

CORNUS
FLORIDA

VINCA
MINOR

Baltic ivy climbs this masonry wall and is controlled with one pruning a year.

To cast pleasing shadows on a wall, this wisteria is being trained to the decorative brackets above. Climbing hydrangea also climbs and clings in the corner and will eventually bear lovely white flowers.

20.
Garden Paths

Whether your property is small or large, do plan a garden walk. This will provide circulation for your property and also make possible an interesting display of plants. A path can be straight as an arrow, follow the contours of the land as it passes through woods, or it can wind up a hillside. A path tends to make a small place seem larger. Wherever it is located, have your path lead somewhere in a leisurely, pleasant way.

A path offers an easy way for you to develop your ideas. By making a path around an old beech tree, hardly noticed before, the tree can become a beautiful feature and the setting for a shady wild-flower garden. I think of one beech which even before the leaves appear is a lovely sight, the ground below carpeted in February with snowdrops, *Galanthus nevalis,* in March with glory-of-the-snow *Chionodoxa,* and in April with the snowflake *Leucojum aestivum.*

On a sunny hillside, let your path wander through the heaths and heathers, *Erica carnea* and *Calluna vulgaris,* which are a mass of color through winter and spring. Plant a path beside a barn with old-fashioned lilacs, their fragrance in May an invitation to walk there.

Width and construction of paths

The width of a garden path depends mainly on its use. Make it at least 3 feet and as much wider as space will allow, even 10 to 12 feet. A path 5 feet wide allows two people to walk comfortably side by side.

The surface material you use depends on where you are building the walk. In the woods pine needles or pine bark make a good covering. A garden path of brick or flagstone is only attractive if it is properly constructed with adequate foundation and drainage. Gravel looks nice when well maintained, and grass is pleasant but will not stand heavy traffic.

Width of borders and plantings

The width of beds bordering a path depends on your design and the existing conditions, also on the plant material you intend to use. Make borders wide, at least 4 feet, and better still 8 to 10 feet to let you include plants of varying heights. Proportion between path and border needs careful consideration. Some borders will be contained by a hedge, others will flow informally into woodland. Designing a path on paper allows you to work out your ideas, get proper proportions, and figure out the number of plants you need.

Select plants for the sides that suit your design and will thrive under the conditions of the site. A path of yellow-flowering plants might begin with winter hazel, *Corylopsis spicata,* and include *C. pauciflora,* forsythia, kerria, and perhaps some of the yellow roses, *Rosa Hugonis,* 'Harison's Yellow' and *R. rugosa* 'Agnes'. Ghent and Mollis azaleas could follow with *Hypericum* for yellow bloom through summer. Or your path might be used to exhibit one kind of flower, as peony or iris. In bloom, the plants would be colorful, and the foliage would be effective the rest of the season.

166

Be sure to plant in groups large enough to make a good showing; avoid isolating a few specimens, particularly if they are edging plants. Work in irregular masses rather than in straight lines. Check all plants for tolerance of shade or sun along your path.

This is most important with ferns for some like sun, others shade. Ferns are invaluable, and just being discovered it would seem. Select those that can be kept in bounds—Christmas, lady, New York, cinnamon, interrupted, and royal. The last three grow tall and should be at the back; hay-scented, sensitive, and ostrich are spreaders. In Chapter 18 on Groundcovers, there is more information on the useful ferns.

Five kinds of junipers—the differences not easy to distinguish in young plants—give variation in height and color along a wide flagstone walk that leads from the house through a sunny area to a viewing terrace overlooking a pond. These are the five: the dwarf *Juniperus chinensis Pfitzeriana nana* and taller *J. Sargentii, J. horizontalis* 'Bar Harbor', *J. plumosa,* and *J. Wiltonii.* As plants mature, texture and color become more pronounced; when they were small, seed of sweet alyssum was scattered among them to give a nice green-and-white pattern that was delightfully fragrant. Summer-flowering shrubs rise in the background.

A rose-bordered flagstone walk connects a large flagstone terrace with a small brick one outside the kitchen. For immediate effect, Floribunda roses in various colors were planted with an edging of white sweet alyssum. The selection of roses is a matter of personal taste with colors, scent, and foliage all to be considered. Each year the American Rose Society offers a "Guide for Buying Roses" (five cents from the Society, 4048 Roselea Place, Columbus, Ohio 43214). Quality ratings are given to help you select the best varieties in each category.

This wide grass walk sets off a collection of dwarf rhododendron and holly. Situated between house and street, spacious plantings on each side include Japanese holly, *Ilex crenata*, trimmed as a tree, and clumps of American holly, *I. opaca*, to give height and background to the lower rhododendrons along the edge of the path. These include the lavender 'Blue Tit', violet-blue 'Blue Diamond', and violet 'Ramapo'. 'Bow Bells' with bright pink flowers offers good contrast. Henry Feil Design

This stepping-stone path leads around the house to the evergreen garden. Myrtle, ivies, and plantain-lilies, *Hosta,* in varieties that bloom for six weeks, make an attractive carpeting below crabapples. Where space is limited, it is often wise to plant groundcovers in this way instead of grass.

An allée of dogwood, planted with trees set 12 feet apart, has an underplanting of myrtle and early spring bulbs. An old Italian jar framed with mountain-laurel terminates this inviting walk. BUHLE PHOTO

Outlining the area between entrance court and rose garden is a wide grass path bordered with lilacs. The June-blooming Japanese tree lilac, *Syringa amurensis japonica,* stands first. Here golden daffodils are followed by the fragrant blossoms of five hybrid lilacs: the single white 'Jan Von Tol', double pink 'Paul Thirion', double sky-blue 'Alphonse Lavalle', double deep blue 'President Viger', and double dark purple 'Night'.

Now the path turns and leads you inside to enjoy your garden from your favorite armchair. I hope these plans and pictures have shown how a good general design and proper selection of plants—along with correct planting and pruning—can make your place more attractive. It has often been said that the more you know about a subject—whether it is painting, music, photography, or cooking—the more you can appreciate its worth. Planting design is no exception.

172

INDEX

181